WHAT TEST-TAKERS ARE SAYING ABOUT LEARNINGEXPRESS PREPARATION GUIDES

"The information from the last two study guides I ordered from your company was invaluable. . . . Better than the $200 6-week study courses being offered. . . . After studying from dozens of books I would choose yours over any of the other companies."

S. Frosch

"Excellent . . . It was like having the test in advance!"

J. Kennedy

"Without this book, I wouldn't have understood the test."

R. Diaz

"Told me everything that was going to be on the test [and] gave me a good understanding of the whole process, too."

J. Molinari

"The best test-prep book I've used!"

H. Hernandez

"I felt 100% prepared when I took the Suffolk County exam this past June. I scored a 96 on it. I had taken it previously in 1992 and only scored an 82. Your guide helped me add 14 points to my score!"

R. Morrell

STATE POLICE CALIFORNIA

HIGHWAY PATROL

LEARNINGEXPRESS

NEW YORK

Copyright © 1996 Learning Express, LLC.

All rights reserved under International and Pan-American Copyright Conventions. Published in the United States by LearningExpress, LLC, New York.

Library of Congress Cataloging-in-Publication Data

Complete preparation guide. California State Police. — 1st ed.

    p.   cm. — (The LearningExpress law enforcement library)

Includes index.

ISBN 1-57685-005-6

    1. Police, State—California—Examinations, questions, etc.   2. Police, State—Vocational guidance—California.   3. Employment tests—California.

I. Series.

HV7571.C2C66   1996

363.2'076—dc20

                                                                       96-11258

                                                                        CIP

Printed in the United States of America

9 8

First Edition

Regarding the Information in this Book

We attempt to verify the information presented in our books prior to publication. It is always a good idea, however, to double-check such important information as minimum requirements, application and testing procedures, and deadlines with your local law enforcement agency, as such information can change from time to time.

For Further Information

For information on LearningExpress, other LearningExpress products, or bulk sales, please call or write to us at:

    LearningExpress™

    900 Broadway

    Suite 604

    New York, NY 10003

    212-995-2566

CONTENTS

LIST OF CONTRIBUTORS

The following individuals contributed to the content of this book.

Susan Camardo is a business and careers writer and communications consultant based in New York City.

Jan Gallagher, Ph.D., is a test-development specialist, editor, and teacher living in Jersey City, New Jersey.

Mary Hesalroad, a former police officer for the Austin, Texas, Police Department, consults with police departments on recruiting efforts and is a freelance writer now living in Alameda, California.

Karen Petty is a New York City-based writer specializing in career development issues.

Judith F. Olson, M.A., is chairperson of the language arts department at Valley High School in West Des Moines, Iowa, where she also conducts test preparation workshops.

Judith Robinovitz is an independent educational consultant and director of Score at the Top, a comprehensive test preparation program in Vero Beach, Florida.

Judith Schlesinger, Ph.D., is a writer and psychologist whose background includes years of working with police officers in psychiatric crisis interventions.

Jay Smith is an exercise physiologist and Director of Physical Fitness and Health Maintenance Programs for the Massachusetts Criminal Justice Training Council.

C · H · A · P · T · E · R 1

THE WORK OF A STATE POLICE OFFICER

CHAPTER SUMMARY

To help you determine if you're ready to make the commitment to become a state police officer, this chapter gives you an overview of what being a trooper is all about. You'll learn about the specific duties and responsibilities of the job, what it's like to be out there every day, what kind of strengths and skills you need, what you can expect to be paid, the upsides—and downsides—of the job, and important issues and trends in the field. And you will get some tips on how to develop a competitive edge before you even start the application process.

T he image of a state police officer is a strong one in the American imagination thanks to countless movies and TV series, from *CHiPs* to *Highway Patrol*, that portray troopers as tough, cool officers in high, shiny boots and impenetrable aviator sunglasses. The day-to-day reality of a state police officer's job, of course, is a lot less glamorous. But it *is* a tough job, requiring physical and mental agility, honesty and integrity, concern and dedication. And it *is* a cool job, because you're performing an important role in our society.

State police officers are known by a number of different names—including state troopers, highway patrol officers, and state traffic officers—and their roster of duties varies from state to state. But the major responsibility that state police officers across the country share is ensuring public safety on their state's roadways. This involves patrolling the highways, enforcing traffic laws, dealing with accidents and other emergencies, assisting motorists, and conducting safety programs.

In addition to highway responsibilities, state police in the majority of states also enforce criminal laws. In communities and counties that do not have a local police force or a large sheriff's department, state troopers are the primary law enforcement agents, investigating crimes such as burglary or assault. They may also help city or county police apprehend lawbreakers and control civil disturbances.

A full 80 percent of all state police forces in the country operated a special drug enforcement unit in 1993. The New York State Police, for example, offers Community Narcotics Enforcement Teams, making undercover troopers and investigators available to work with local law enforcement agencies. In 1992, its members worked with local police in Buffalo in an operation that led to the arrest of nearly 100 drug dealers and customers—one of the biggest roundups of street-level criminals in New York State history. (For specific duties related to state police officers, see sidebar on next page.)

All states except Hawaii have some type of statewide police force. Fourteen states, mostly in the west and south, have highway patrols, 27 have state police departments, and eight have departments of public safety.

JUST THE FACTS
The first modern statewide police agency was the Pennsylvania State Constabulary, established in 1905.

Demographics, Salary and Job Security

There were approximately 52,000 full-time sworn state police officers in the United States in 1993. This still tends to be a man's world—95 percent of these state officers were male. The force with the largest percentage of female troopers was the Wisconsin State Patrol, with 12.4 percent, followed by the Michigan State Police (9.7 percent) and the Florida Highway Patrol (9.4 percent). The North Carolina State Highway Patrol employed the least percentage of women (0.6 percent). State police forces also tend to be predominantly white. The average percent of white state police officers in 1993 was 89 percent; 7 percent were black, 3 percent Hispanic, and 1 percent other races.

The pay of a state police officer varies widely, but on average, the base annual starting salary of an entry-level officer in 1993 was $23,300. The states paying the highest to troopers just starting out were Alaska ($42,192) and California ($35,016). The lowest-paying states were Vermont ($18,720) and Wyoming ($18,828). As far as benefits go, state troopers often get a package that includes such standard elements as vacation, sick leave, holiday, and overtime pay; insurance (life, medical and disability); a uniform allowance; tuition reimbursement; and a retirement plan.

Since the public sector, like so many other employers, has been "downsizing" in recent years, what's the job outlook for state police officers? The Bureau of Labor Statistics projects that the employment of all types

Specific Duties of State Troopers

While the activities of state troopers vary from state to state, here are some of the specific duties they may be called on to perform:

- Patroling state and interstate highways
- Enforcing motor vehicle and criminal laws
- Monitoring traffic to: arrest or issue tickets or warnings to those violating motor vehicle regulations and safe driving practices, including speeding and driving while intoxicated; identify unsafe vehicles; detect stolen vehicles
- Providing information and assistance to motorists
- Observing and reporting public safety hazards, such as obstacles in the road or unsafe driving conditions
- Directing activities at the site of accidents or emergencies
- Providing first aid
- Investigating conditions and causes of accidents
- Directing traffic in congested areas
- Serving as escort for officials and dignitaries, funerals, processions, military convoys, parades
- Appearing in court as a witness in traffic violation and criminal cases
- Keeping records and making reports regarding activities, such as daily patrol occurrences or ongoing investigations
- Assisting law enforcement officers not under state jurisdiction
- Conducting safety programs for the public and at schools
- Inspecting automobiles and school buses for safe operating conditions
- Enforcing commercial vehicle weight laws
- Conducting driver exams

of police officers is expected to increase through the year 2005. An increasingly fearful society is demanding more police protection of all kinds. But employment growth will be tempered by continuing budgetary constraints faced by law enforcement agencies in many states. Turnover in police jobs is among the lowest of all occupations, and most job openings come from the need to replace retiring officers.

Rewards and Risks

State police officers, like other law enforcement officials, have one of the most challenging yet rewarding jobs in our society. Being a state trooper offers you the chance to do responsible, worthwhile work. Each day holds the promise of making a positive difference in people's lives, right on up to saving lives. Other pluses include the variety of duties you perform and the personal challenges you undergo. It's also a profession known for a great spirit of camaraderie. State troopers are enormously proud of the work they do, and strongly supportive of each other.

But there's another, darker side to the job of a state police officer. While most days are quiet "business as usual" times, there is always the threat of danger. Random acts of violence, fueled by ready access to guns and drugs, have become daily occurrences and number among the expected crimes that a state trooper must confront. High-speed car chases are certainly not the norm, but when they do occur there's the possibility of cars crashing and burning.

Unfortunately, the injury rate among law enforcement officers is higher than in many occupations and reflects the risks taken in pursuing speeding motorists, apprehending criminals and dealing with emergencies. And even when state police officers aren't directly in harm's way, they often have to perform duties that are difficult or unpleasant, such as confronting a driver under the influence of drugs or alcohol, or heartbreaking, like assisting at a bloody accident scene.

Stress is a way of life for the state police officer as well as for his/her family. And this stress comes from a number of sources—the danger inherent in this line of work; a changing schedule that disrupts sleeping habits as well as family and social life; dealing with the perception of some citizens that law enforcement officials of all kinds are corrupt or racist. And since state troopers are as human as the next person, there is a tendency to take these tensions home, which can sometimes lead to additional problems.

It's important to think about this tough side of state policing if you plan to enter the field. But remember, too, that there's a lot of support available to help troopers handle the pressures of the job. Many departments actively provide training and assistance, ranging from stress management programs to confidential counseling services. And you can also rely on fellow troopers for understanding and encouragement. They, better than anyone else, know how stressful state police work can be.

A Day in the Life

Now that you have an idea of "the big picture," you probably want to know what it's like to be a state police officer on a day-to-day basis.

State police officers generally work a basic five-day, 40-hour week, with rotating shifts. Some states (New Jersey, for instance) use a "4/10" shift rotation—four days a week, 10 hours a day, which many troopers find better for their health and productivity. Since protection is needed on a 24-hour basis, you'll sometimes have to work nights, weekends and holidays. You may be required to work overtime, and you have to be prepared to be on call any time your services are needed.

Most troopers patrol the highways and byways of their states in cars and motorcycles, although some use planes, helicopters, and even boats. While you may be working with a partner, the great majority of state police (94 percent, according to a 1993 survey) go on patrol alone. If you're a "road dog" you don't have much direct supervision, but troopers are continually in contact with their communications centers to check in with superiors and receive orders. You have to be prepared to work outdoors for long periods of time in all kinds of weather. And you will be required to wear—and must be prepared to use—a gun.

While most of your daily duties will be routine—such as clocking the speed of passing vehicles or helping motorists—at some point you're likely to encounter more dramatic situations. Some state troopers have delivered babies, others have stopped people from committing suicide. But sometimes a trooper is not able to save lives. State police officers are among the first to arrive at the scene of a highway accident. At these times, you will have to be the ultimate professional, providing emergency care, gathering evidence on the cause of the accident, and helping others to cope.

HAVE YOU GOT WHAT IT TAKES?

To perform successfully as a state police officer, you need to possess several different kinds of strengths. First, there's physical ability. You have to stay in excellent shape and be ready to handle a variety of situations that require strength, endurance and agility.

Emotional stability and good character are also critical. Anyone in this line of work must clearly have a sense of responsibility and respect for authority. A good state trooper needs to be fair and open-minded, honest, even-tempered, tactful, quick-thinking, disciplined and self-confident. He or she must be able to make decisions independently, cope with high levels of stress, and exercise sound judgment.

State police should enjoy working with people and serving the public from all walks of life—of every race, religion, sex, sexual preference, age or socioeconomic class. And they are obligated to treat all people equally and equitably under the law.

Important Skills to Develop

In addition, a top-notch trooper possesses a number of other qualities that enhance his or her ability to get the job done well. These include:

- *Good oral and written communication skills.* State police work involves a constant processing of information, both spoken and written. Troopers are called on to deal with all kinds of people in all kinds of situations. In the course of a day, you may have to stop a speeding driver, help a distraught motorist stranded on the road, or testify in a court case. In each of these very different situations, you have to be able to express yourself in an appropriate and effective manner. The ability to write clearly and concisely is also important, since state police officers continually file detailed reports that may become legal evidence in a court case.

- *Good observation skills.* As a state police officer, you will be expected to accurately report on what you see and hear at the scene of an accident or arrest. This includes being able to draw accurate sketches of accident scenes. Your ability to notice and remember telling details can be very important in conducting investigations, writing reports, and testifying in court cases. It's also very useful to be alert in picking up on suspicious behavior.

- *Good driving skills.* Many state police officers spend most of their time on the road, sometimes in hazardous weather conditions or high-speed pursuits. The better your driving skills, the more safely and adeptly you will be able to handle these situations.

THE APPLICATION PROCESS

If what you've read so far appeals to you, and you think you've got the right stuff to be a state trooper, it's time to think about what's involved in applying for the job. Typical basic requirements you need to be aware of include:

- A minimum age, usually between 18 and 21
- Excellent health and good vision and hearing
- U.S. citizenship; most states also have a residency requirement
- A high school diploma or its equivalent; some states have a higher education requirement
- A valid driver's license for the state
- A clean criminal record

In Chapter 2, you'll find the specifics of how state troopers in your state are selected. But briefly, here's what you can expect:

- A written exam that typically tests such areas as reading comprehension, observation and memory, and communication skills
- A thorough medical exam
- Various tests of physical ability
- A psychological or personality evaluation
- A thorough background investigation
- An oral interview with a panel of state police officers

- In some states, drug testing and a polygraph (lie detector) test

Like other kinds of law enforcement work, state policing is an attractive career option to many people, and the number of qualified candidates often exceeds the number of job openings in some state police departments. In Texas, for example, the Department of Public Safety hadn't done any hiring between 1990 and 1994. So when hiring resumed, the DPS was deluged with 9,000 applications for 130 positions. With competition this tough, it helps to get any kind of edge you can. (See sidebar for suggestions.)

Gaining That Competitive Edge

Competition for state police jobs is tough, so any special abilities or experiences you offer could be to your advantage in getting accepted as a new recruit. Here are some areas that may prove useful to develop:

- **Education**. All state police departments require at least a high school diploma. But recently, an increasing number of states are asking for at least some college training. In 1993, 4 percent of state police agencies required a four-year college degree, 10 percent wanted a two-year college degree, and 14 percent had a nondegree college requirement. Whatever the requirement in your state, it can't hurt to go beyond it. It would be particularly useful to explore programs in such relevant fields as law enforcement, criminal justice, or political science. Other courses helpful in preparing for a state police career include psychology, counseling, English, American history, public administration, public relations, sociology, law, chemistry and physics.

- **Second Languages**. Being able to speak and/or write more than one language can be an asset. This is especially true in areas that have large concentrations of ethnic populations. Communicating with non-English-speaking people in their native language can be a big help in assisting motorists and conducting investigations. And it could save your life in certain threatening situations.

- **Computer Skills**. In state policing, as in just about every other occupation, computer literacy is becoming critical as electronic communication and record-keeping becomes the norm — not only at headquarters, but from your police car as well. For example, a patrol car equipped with a mobile digital terminal or notebook computer may allow officers to tap into state or national data bases to run checks on drivers, vehicles, weapons or records, or to send inquiries via electronic mail ("e-mail"). Completing routine reports on a computer can also save a lot of time. When computers are networked or linked to a mainframe at the department, this "paperwork" can then go directly into the main electronic files for storage.

WHEN YOU'VE MADE THE GRADE

When you meet all the requirements of the state police agency to which you're applying, your name is added to a list of eligible candidates. Recruits are chosen from this list as vacancies open up in the ranks. How quickly you make it from the list to the force varies from state to state and can be affected by budgetary considerations.

New recruits undergo extremely rigorous formal training that often lasts several months. The program at the state police academy in New York, for instance, runs for 24 weeks, while the one in California goes 27 weeks. Trooper trainees usually receive instruction in such areas as criminal law and state motor vehicle codes; laws and procedures concerning arrest, search and seizure; traffic control and accident prevention; investigation methods; ethics; communications; community relations; use of firearms; self-defense; high-speed driving; first aid; and handling emergencies. In 1993, the median number of classroom training hours required for new state police officers was 800, while the median number of field training hours was 320.

Once you've successfully completed your training, you'll be assigned to duty, usually working with veteran officers until you learn the ropes. Keep in mind that for your first duty, you could be stationed anywhere in the state, not necessarily in the area in which you currently live. You'll be serving on a probationary basis for a period of anything from six months to a year or more, depending on the state. After that, if your work is satisfactory, your employment becomes permanent.

Moving On—and Up

As you move on in your career, you'll find that many state police departments help troopers to keep up with the latest in law enforcement and improve their job performance by offering ongoing training programs in a variety of areas. These range from super-visory training to seminars in criminal investigative techniques to courses on ethics, human relations and communications.

While many state troopers enjoy being out in the field handling a wide variety of duties, some choose to specialize in a particular function. In many states there may be opportunities in such areas as training new recruits, fingerprint analysis, ballistics testing, and laboratory analysis of criminal evidence.

When it comes to moving up the career ladder, promotions are generally made based on job performance and scoring on a written examination. The ranks you can aspire to include Corporal, Sergeant, First Sergeant, Lieutenant, Captain, Major, Inspector, Deputy Superintendent, and Superintendent. (Titles or rankings may differ by state.) Anyone who meets the qualifications for a higher position can take the promotional exam for it.

> JUST THE FACTS
> **The National Uniform Manufacturers Association, which holds a contest each year for best uniform, named the Connecticut State Police as the best-dressed law enforcement officers in the country in 1995.**

ISSUES AND TRENDS

As an aspiring state police officer, you'll want to keep on top of what's going on in the country, and especially your state, that could have an impact on the way troopers do their job. There are a number of "hot" issues and trends in the field of law enforcement and criminal justice that are likely to be commanding attention for some time to come.

Recent opinion polls and election results have indicated loud and clear that the public is saying get tough on crime. Crime is one of the most serious social issues of the day, and people are becoming ever more fearful about the proliferation of drug- and gang-related violence in our communities. So you know that the kind of work state police officers are doing is ever more important in our society.

But at the same time that the public wants stronger law enforcement, many citizens seem to have lost respect for the officers who do the enforcing. Recent high-profile trials, such as those of O.J. Simpson and the officers accused of beating Rodney King, were accompanied by endless commentary about the questionable conduct of some police officers. While these cases didn't involve state troopers, all law enforcement officers have been affected, as many citizens have lost faith in the men and women sworn to protect them. This negative attitude can be very demoralizing for a state police officer who is putting his or her life on the line every day—not to mention possible departmental or legal inquiry if their actions are questioned.

High-Tech Tools for the Next Century

On a more positive note, troopers are getting state-of-the-art tools that are helping them to do their jobs more quickly and efficiently. In particular, state police departments are rapidly pulling onto the information superhighway with the increasing use of computers. In 1993, state police agencies most frequently used computers for such routine functions as record-keeping, fleet management, and budgeting. But a significant number also used them for crime investigation (63 percent) and analysis (45 percent).

And many states are now taking the next high-tech step forward, installing computers in patrol cars. This is a real boon to troopers, making it much easier for them to communicate with each other, conduct immediate vehicle and criminal checks, and perform routine paperwork. The Washington State Patrol, for example, recently equipped many of its cruisers with a 486 notebook computer with a 120-megabyte hard disk drive, modem and two-way radio. So in a few years, it's likely that computer literacy will not just be an advantage for aspiring state troopers, but a necessity.

MAKING THE COMMITMENT

If you're determined to carve out a career for yourself as a state police officer, do yourself a favor and start to prepare *now*, regardless of when the next exam is scheduled. Here are some actions you can take to get going:

- *Get fit.* Working out regularly and participating in sports will help you develop the strength, stamina and agility needed for state police work. Try enrolling in martial arts classes. Martial arts are valuable not only for their practical techniques of self-defense, but also for their mind/body connection that can help you remain centered and focused under stressful circumstances.

- *Conduct your own background investigation.* Go to the library and go online to read all you can about law enforcement in general and state policing in particular. Many police organizations and government agencies publish newsletters that are available to non-members. The criminal justice departments of colleges and universities are a good source of books, newsletters, academic papers, and research reports. Call the public information office of the state police in the state(s) you're interested in and see if they have a brochure, annual report or press kit to send you.

Read the paper daily to keep up not only on news about state police officers and departments, but also on social issues, legal matters and new laws, crime trends and other areas that directly affect state police work. If you have access to a computer and can get on the Internet, you'll find a wealth of material on law enforcement. (See sidebar for an introductory guide to going online.)

- *Do some networking.* The best way to learn about what it's like to be a state trooper is to talk to people who are on the force. If you don't know anyone, ask family, friends and acquaintances if *they* know someone—word will get around and the chances are that sooner or later you'll be able to identify someone who can answer your questions and give you some pointers. You can also make friends in cyberspace—there are a number of online discussion groups in the law enforcement area, and at least one dedicated specifically to state troopers (see sidebar).

Resources in Cyberspace

If you have a computer and access to online services and the Internet, there are plenty of places to find out more about the field of law enforcement. Here are just a few of them:

- ***State Troopers Forum.*** America Online (AOL) carries this bulletin board/discussion group, which features lively contributions from state police officers, "wanna-be" troopers, and interested citizens from all over the country. The postings range from fun (a raucous report on a recent regional picnic) to sadly serious (announcements of troopers who have died in the line of duty). This forum is frequented by a lot of people who want to become state troopers, seeking advice on everything from the testing dates and hiring situations in particular states to what to expect on the exams and interviews. The troopers who participate tend to be very proud of their profession and supportive of each other and those interested in joining their ranks. [AOL path: Clubs and Interests/Professional Organizations/Public Safety/1st Precinct/State Troopers Forum]

- ***Law Enforcement Sites on the Web.*** This site is billed as "possibly the largest collection of law enforcement sites on the Web." That's the plus side—you can access all the other sites from here. However, precisely because it's so thorough, it can be time-consuming to work with. A search function helps, allowing you to confine your travels by giving key words that describe your particular interests. [URL address: http://www.geopages.com/CapitolHill/1814/ira.html]

- ***Cecil Greek's Criminal Justice Page.*** Created by a professor of criminal justice at the University of Southern Florida, this site features law enforcement sites as well as links to judicial, legal, correctional/penal and education sites and various on-line magazines (or "e-zines") on the Web. The wide range of subjects covered include current court cases, drugs and alcohol, terrorism, juvenile delinquency, and the death penalty. You can also check out the Most Wanted List, trial photos, and actual forensic photos. [URL address: http://www.stpt.usf.edu/~greek/cj.html]

- ***Cop Net & Police Resource List.*** The wealth of information provided on this site includes links to state police departments and other types of law enforcement agencies as well as diverse public information and law enforcement association sites. [URL address: http://police.sas.ab.ca]

- *Get ready for the written exam.* In general, the written exam will gauge your skills in such areas as logical reasoning, good judgment, problem-solving, observation and memory for details, basic grammar and writing skills, and reading comprehension. Don't wait until the night before the test to start getting ready. The more you prepare, the more relaxed and confident you'll be when you actually sit down to take the exam.

- *Prepare for the oral interview.* A lot of people become shy and self-conscious talking about their background, skills and ambitions with a stranger. But you're going to have to do that—and convincingly—when you go through the interview that is part of the application process. Thinking about your answers beforehand may help to reduce your anxiety about the interview process. Why do you want to become a state trooper? What are your goals on the force? What kind of knowledge, abilities and experiences do you bring to the job? Once you've put your answers into words—even writing them down, if that helps—practice telling them to someone else—a friend or family member, perhaps. The idea is not to have memorized or "canned" responses, but to be clear about your choice, your potential and your talents so you feel comfortable talking about them.

It takes deep dedication and a lot of hard work to become a state police officer. But those who have made it through the arduous application process and the tough training to join the elite world of state troopers think it's worth the effort—to hear them talk, they have the best job in the world. If you think you've got what it takes, give it all you've got.

STATE POLICE OFFICER SUITABILITY TEST

CHAPTER SUMMARY

Wanting to be a state police officer is one thing; being suited for it is something else. The following self-quiz can help you decide whether you and this career make a good match.

There is no one "type" of person who becomes a state police officer. State troopers are as varied as any any other group of people in their personalities, experiences, and styles. At the same time, there are some attitudes and behaviors that seem to predict success and satisfaction in this profession. They have nothing to do with your intelligence and ability—they simply reflect how you interact with other people, and how you choose to approach the world.

These "suitability factors" were pulled from research literature and discussions with police psychologists, trainers and screeners. They fall into five groups; each has ten questions spaced throughout the test.

The State Police Officer Suitability Test is not a formal psychological test. For one thing, it's not nearly long enough; the MMPI (Minnesota Multiphasic Personality Inventory) test used in most psychological assessments has 11 times more items than this test. For another, it does not focus on your general mental health.

Instead, the test should be viewed as an informal guide—a private tool to help you decide whether being a state police officer would suit you, and whether you would enjoy it. It also provides the opportunity for greater self-understanding, which is beneficial no matter what you do for a living.

STATE POLICE OFFICER SUITABILITY TEST

DIRECTIONS

You'll need about 20 minutes to answer the 50 questions below. It's a good idea to do them all at one sitting—scoring and interpretation can be done later. For each question, consider how often the attitude or behavior applies to you. You have a choice between Never, Rarely, Sometimes, Often, and Always; put the number for your answer in the space after each question. For example, if the answer is "sometimes," the score for that item is 10; "always" gets a 40, etc. How they add up will be explained later. If you try to outsmart the test, or figure out the "right" answers, you won't get an accurate picture at the end. So just be honest.

PLEASE NOTE: Don't read the scoring sections before you answer the questions, or you'll defeat the whole purpose of the exercise!

How often do the following statements sound like you? Choose one answer for each statement.

NEVER	RARELY	SOMETIMES	OFTEN	ALWAYS
0	5	10	20	40

1. I like to know what's expected of me. ____

2. I am willing to admit my mistakes to other people. ____

3. Once I've made a decision, I stop thinking about it. ____

4. I can shrug off my fears about getting physically hurt. ____

5. It's important to know what to expect. ____

6. It takes a lot to get me really angry. ____

7. My first impressions of people tend to be accurate. ____

8. I rely on my sense of humor. ____

9. I like to take control of confused situations. ____

10. I enjoy working with others. ____

11. I trust my instincts. ____

12. I enjoy being teased. ____

13. I will spend as much time as it takes to settle a disagreement. ____

14. I feel comfortable talking to strangers. ____

15. I dislike taking risks. ____

16. I'm in a good mood. ____

17. I'm comfortable making quick decisions when necessary. ____

18. Rules must be obeyed, even if you don't agree with them. ____

19. It's important to be respected. ____

20. I like working alone. ____

21. I stay away from doing exciting things that I know are dangerous. ____

22. I don't mind when a boss tells me what to do. ____

23. I enjoy solving puzzles. ____

24. The people I know consult me about their problems. ____

25. I am comfortable making my own decisions. ____

26. I like things to be consistent and structured. ____

27. When I get stressed, I can make myself relax. ____

28. I have confidence in my own common sense. ____

29. I make my friends laugh. ____

30. When I make a promise, I keep it. ____

31. When I'm in a group, I tend to be the leader. ____

32. I can stay cool in tense situations. ____

33. When I get into a fight, I can stop myself from losing control. ____

34. It's good to have rules. ____

35. I understand why I do the things I do. ____

36. I'm good at calming people down. ____

37. I can tell how people are feeling even when they don't say anything. ____

38. I take criticism without getting upset. ____

39. People follow my advice. ____

40. It's important that other people respect my judgment. ____

41. I try to make a good impression. ____

42. I remember to show up on time. ____

43. I like to have guidelines to follow. ____

44. I plan what I'm going to do next. ____

45. Being admired is important to me. ____

46. People see me as a very calm person. ____

47. It's more important for me to do a good job than to get praised for it. ____

48. I prefer to "go by the book" in making decisions. ____

49. I like things to be neat. ____

50. I take responsibility for my own actions rather than blame others. ____

SCORING

Attitudes and behaviors can't be measured in units, like distance or weight. Besides, psychological categories tend to overlap. As a result, the numbers and dividing lines between score ranges are approximate, and numbers may vary about 20 points either way. If your score doesn't fall in the optimal range, it doesn't mean a "failure"—only an area that needs focus.

It may help to share your results with some of the people who are close to you. Very often, there are differences between how we see ourselves and how we actually come across to others.

GROUP 1 – RISK

Add up scores for questions 4, 6, 12, 15, 21, 27, 33, 38, 44, and 46

TOTAL = _____

This group evaluates your tendency to be assertive and take risks. The ideal is in the middle, somewhere between timid and reckless: you should be willing to take risks, but not seek them out just for excitement. Being nervous, impulsive, and afraid of physical injury are all undesirable traits for a state police officer; it is important to stay calm under fire, which can include criticism and teasing by superiors, colleagues and the public. And as you can imagine, it's important for someone who carries a gun to be able to exercise self-control when under stress.

- If you score between 200 and 400, you are on the right track.
- A score between 100 and 200 suggests a kind of macho approach that can be dangerous in the field. As one state police officer trainer put it, "we don't want crash dummies wearing the uniform."

- A score below 100 indicates that the more dangerous and stressful aspects of the job would be difficult for you; after all, the single most dangerous law enforcement activity is the traffic stop.

GROUP 2 – CORE

Add up scores for questions 2, 8, 16, 19, 26, 30, 35, 42, 47, and 50

TOTAL = _____

This group reflects such basic traits as stability, reliability, and self-awareness. Can your fellow officers count on you to do your part when backup may be miles away? Are you secure enough to do your job without needing praise? Remember that state police officers work alone—except for the graveyard shift—so you must be able to appreciate your own efforts.

It is crucial to be able to admit your mistakes and take responsibility for your actions, to be confident without being arrogant or conceited, and to communicate clearly and with authority. In a job where lives are at stake, both the rules and the facts must be clear. Mood is also very important. While we all have good and bad days, someone who is depressed much of the time is not encouraged to pursue police work; depression affects one's judgment, energy level, and the ability to respond and communicate.

- If you score between 170 and 400, you're in the ballpark.
- A score of 100-170 indicates you should look at the questions again and evaluate your style of social interaction.
- Scores below 100 suggest that you may not be ready for this job—yet.

GROUP 3 – JUDGMENT

Add scores for questions 3, 7, 11, 17, 23, 28, 37, 40, 43, and 48

TOTAL = ____

This group taps how you make decisions. Successful state police officers are sensitive to unspoken messages, can detect and respond to other people's feelings, and make fair and accurate assessments of a situation, rather than being influenced by their own personal biases and needs. Once the decision to act is made, second-guessing can be dangerous. State police officers must make their best judgments in line with accepted practices, and then act upon these judgments without hesitancy or self-doubt. Such confidence is essential when there is no partner to consult—which is most of the time. Finally, it's important to accept that you cannot change the world single-handedly. People who seek this career because they want to make a dramatic individual difference in human suffering are likely to be frustrated and disappointed.

- If you scored between 200 and 400, your style of making decisions, especially about people, fits with the desired profile.
- Scores between 100 and 200 suggest that you think about how you make judgments and how much confidence you have in them.
- If you scored below 100, you may want to re-evaluate whether you and this career would make a good match.

GROUP 4 – AUTHORITY

Add scores for questions 1, 10, 13, 18, 22, 25, 31, 34, 39, and 45

TOTAL = ____

This group contains the vital attributes of respect for rules and authority—including the "personal authority" of self-reliance and leadership—and the ability to resolve conflict. State police officers must accept and communicate the value of structure and control without being rigid. And while most decisions are made independently, the authority of the supervisor and the law must be obeyed at all times; following the rules is crucial when alone in the field. Finally, anyone on a personal mission for justice or vengeance is not welcome in law enforcement, and is unlikely to make it through the screening process.

- A score between 180 and 400 indicates you have the desired attitude toward authority—both your own and that of your superior officers.
- If you scored between 100 and 180, you might think about whether a solitary leadership role is something you want every day.
- Below 100—ask yourself whether the combination of extreme structure and independence would be comfortable for you.

GROUP 5 – STYLE
Add up scores for questions 5, 9, 14, 20, 24, 29, 32, 36, 41, and 49

TOTAL = _____

This is the personal style dimension which describes how you come across to others. State police officers should be seen as strong and capable, but not dramatic or heavy-handed; friendly, but not overly concerned with whether they are liked; patient, but not to the point of losing control of a situation. A good sense of humor is essential, not only in the field but also among one's fellow officers. Other desirable qualities include consistency tempered with flexibility, the ability to calm people down, and knowing how to make a good impression—communicating that "non-verbal command presence" that state police officers need to possess.

- A score between 200 and 400 is optimal.
- Scores between 100 and 200 suggest that you compare your style with the above description and consider whether anything needs to be modified.
- If you scored below 100, you might think about the way you interact with others and whether you'd be happy in a job where taking charge is the main focus.

SUMMARY

The State Police Officer Suitability Test reflects the fact that being a successful state police officer requires moderation and consistency, rather than extremes. Attitudes that are desirable in reasonable amounts can become a real problem if they are too strong. For example, independence is essential, but too much of it creates a "Dirty Harry" type who takes the law into his or her own hands. State police officers must make strong, confident decisions that are strictly in line with procedure and based on accurate judgments about the people they encounter. They must project an image that commands respect without having to say a word.

As one police trainer said, the ideal officer is "low key and low maintenance." Excitable people who are unsure of themselves do not make good state police officers; neither do those who prefer to improvise rather than follow the rules. Keep this in mind as you look at your scores.

This test was developed by Judith Schlesinger, Ph.D., a writer and psychologist whose background includes years of working with police officers in psychiatric crisis interventions.

C · H · A · P · T · E · R

BECOMING A CALIFORNIA HIGHWAY PATROL OFFICER

3

CHAPTER SUMMARY

This chapter describes in detail the selection process for becoming a State Traffic Officer in California. It offers the applicant useful information in such key areas as requirements and procedures, training, salary and benefits, and initial assignment.

T
he Department of California Highway Patrol, known as the CHP, is the largest state law enforcement agency in the U.S. In 1995, in an effort to streamline state government and increase the efficiency of providing safety to the public, the California State Police (CSP) merged with the Department of California Highway Patrol. The combined ranks of sworn personnel now total almost 6,000.

Traditionally, the CHP, which gained national recognition with the long-running television series "CHiPs," is responsible for the patrol and safety of California highways and the enforcement of state traffic laws. When the departments merged, CHP incorporated into its jurisdiction the duties formerly handled by the CSP, such as patrol and protection of certain state buildings and protection of high-level state government officials such as the governor.

IMPORTANT ADDRESSES & PHONE NUMBERS

Mail applications to:
California Highway Patrol
Selection Standards and
Examinations Section
860 Stillwater Road
West Sacramento, CA 95605-1649
916-375-2535

Recruitment Unit
916-375-2548
1-888-4A CHP JOB
e-mail: recruiting@chp.ca.gov
website: www.chp.ca.gov/recruiting/recruiting.html

(continued)

IMPORTANT ADDRESSES & PHONE NUMBERS (CONTINUED)

California Highway Patrol
Academy
3500 Reed Avenue
West Sacramento, CA 95605
916-372-5620

State Personnel Board Medical
Officer
P.O. Box 944201
Sacramento, CA 94244-2010
916-653-0790

For examination information:
State Personnel Board Office
916-653-1705

In addition to traffic patrol, the CHP reinforces county sheriff departments in emergencies and in large-scale investigations. The CHP also provides protection to visiting dignitaries, while its mounted police division and bicycle unit patrol the state capitol grounds in Sacramento.

The California Highway Patrol has developed the following statement of its mission to the State of California:

The primary mission of the Department is the management and regulation of traffic to achieve safe, lawful and efficient use of the highway transportation system.

APPLYING TO BECOME AN OFFICER IN THE CALIFORNIA HIGHWAY PATROL

MINIMUM REQUIREMENTS

To apply for the entry-level position of Cadet, California Highway Patrol in California, you must meet the minimum requirements described below.

Education

At the time of the written test date, you must have either a high school diploma, a General Educational Development diploma (GED) or have passed a high school proficiency examination. CHP values applicants who have higher education and foreign language skills.

If you are a pilot and wish to use this skill in your work, you must possess a FAA Commercial Pilot's Certificate, Airplane or Rotorcraft Helicopter, and a current Class II medical certificate. You must show documentation of instrument rating and have logged 500 hours as pilot-in-command.

Age

To participate in the examination process, you must be between 20 and 31 years old. However, you cannot be appointed unless you are at least 21 years old.

Citizenship

If you are a permanent resident alien who is eligible for and has applied for citizenship, you may compete in the examination process. To be appointed, you must be a U.S. citizen.

Health

You must be free from any physical, mental or emotional problems that may prevent you from fulfilling all the duties of the job. Your health and overall physical condition must be good and must conform to the following standards:

CALIFORNIA HIGHWAY PATROL: AT A GLANCE

Full-Time Sworn State Traffic Officers	4,856
Females	444
Caucasians	3,737
African-Americans	193
Hispanics	733
Asians	96
Filipinos	47
Native Americans	5
Pacific Islanders	21
Other	24
Full-Time State Traffic Officers Hired in 1995	508
Applicants for Full-Time Sworn State Traffic Officer in 1995	38,000
Average Age of Police Officer Recruits	25
Average Age at Retirement	52

Note: Figures supplied by the California Highway Patrol, Personnel and Training Department.

- weight proportionate to your age and height
- height not more than six feet six inches
- normal hearing ability
- uncorrected vision no worse than 20/40 in each eye corrected to 20/20 in each eye, with no visual abnormalities, such as color blindness

Criminal Record

To apply for this position you must have a satisfactory record as a law-abiding citizen. Your driving and criminal records are examined. Felony convictions are cause for automatic disqualification, with the exception of certain convictions involving marijuana. Contact the CHP Recruiting Unit or the Selection Standards Section for further details on these exceptions.

Driver's License

You must possess a valid California driver's license at the time of appointment. When necessary, you receive on-the-job motorcycle training.

Other

Other personal characteristics the CHP finds desirable in applicants are:

- an interest in law enforcement work
- willingness to work throughout the state and at unusual hours
- willingness to learn to operate a motorcycle
- keenness of observation
- honesty
- tact
- reliability
- maturity
- neat personal appearance

SELECTION PROCESS

The selection process for becoming a State Traffic Officer Cadet consists of six steps, each of which assesses a certain aspect of your ability and character. You must successfully complete each step, which usually follow in this order:

1. Application
2. Written Examination and essay test
3. Physical Ability Test
4. Qualifications Appraisal Interview
5. Background Investigation
6. Psychological Examination
7. Medical Examination

If you successfully complete the written exam, physical ability test and qualifications appraisal interview, your name is put on an eligibility list. You must pass all phases of the process before you are appointed to the Academy. Note that these steps are subject to change. According to the CHP, you will be notified of any changes in the selection process.

If you are a disabled veteran, you may receive an additional 15 Veteran's Preference points on your examination score. Other veterans, as well as widows or widowers of veterans and spouses of 100% disabled veterans, are granted 10 additional points.

Step One: Application

If you meet the minimum qualifications listed above, you may submit an application for the written examination. Applications can be obtained from the State Personnel Board office in Sacramento or you may call the number listed at the beginning of this chapter. After you have obtained and completed the application, mail it to the CHP Selection Standards and Examinations Section. You are notified of your examination and interview dates by mail.

A copy of the application form is presented at the end of this chapter. While you can't submit the application presented here, you *can* use this copy to practice filling out the form and to see firsthand what you'll be asked to provide.

....

IMPORTANT

You must bring one piece of photo identification or two forms of signed identification to be admitted into all test sites.

....

Step Two: Written Examination

The written examination is offered at sites throughout the state. The exam tests your ability to read and understand written communications and evaluates your writing ability, including spelling and grammar. This test is graded on a pass/fail basis, a passing score being 70 percent or higher.

Step Three: Physical Ability Test

If you pass the written exam, you are scheduled for a Physical Ability Test (P.A.T.). The following five exercises measure your physical strength, endurance and flexibility:

- *500-Yard Run*
  You must run 500 yards in two minutes or less.
- *Upper Body Strength*
  You must pass a shoulder strength test, a grip strength test, and a test in which you pedal a stationary bicycle for up to one minute.
- *Trunk Strength Flexion*
  This test requires you to exert 113 pounds of force by using your abdominal muscles.
- *Side Step*
  In this test, you must stand astride a line with your feet parallel. You are required to sidestep over the line with your right foot, crossing the line, then with the left foot. A point is scored for each time you step over the line and you must score 13 points in 10 seconds.
- *100-Yard Sprint*
  You must run 100 yards in 20 seconds or less.

The California Highway Patrol offers a brochure that describes a training program designed to prepare candidates for the P.A.T. You may obtain this brochure by contacting the CHP Health and Safety Section at the number listed at the beginning of this chapter.

If you are taking any prescribed medications at the time of the P.A.T., it is recommended that you consult your physician before taking this test.

Step Four: Qualifications Appraisal Interview

The fourth step in the selection process is an interview, which assesses readiness for a career in law enforcement. The interview evaluates your ability to:

- accurately analyze a situation and take an effective course of action
- take on the obligations, responsibility and conditions of employment of a State Traffic Officer Cadet
- deal with problems effectively and tactfully
- use sound judgment
- understand and relate ideas with directness and clarity

Step Five: Background Investigation

The background investigation is an extensive check into your criminal, driving, educational, financial, employment, and related histories. You provide this information to CHP on a form, which you receive earlier in the selection process. Fingerprints of all candidates are taken at the time of the background investigation.

Step Six: Psychological Evaluation

The psychological evaluation verifies that you are free from any mental or emotional condition that may impair your ability to function as a State Traffic Officer. You take a written test and attend an interview with a clinical psychologist or physician.

Step Seven: Medical Examination

Before you are hired by the CHP, you must pass a complete medical examination. This exam is performed by a licensed physician and determines that you have no physical problems that may limit your capacity to perform all the duties of the position. Such problems may be a bad back, problems with digestion, cardiovascular abnormality, or pelvic bone or tissue abnormality.

You are required to undergo a drug test as part of the process and any positive results are cause for immediate disqualification.

If you successfully complete all phases of the selection process and your name is chosen from the eligibility list, you begin training as a State Traffic Officer Cadet.

TRAINING

State Traffic Officer Cadet training is conducted at the Department of California Highway Patrol Training Academy in Sacramento. The 1400-hour training program lasts 26 weeks and encompasses 94 subject areas, including:

- Domestic Violence
- Crimes in Progress
- Community Relations
- Criminal Law
- Traffic Laws and Regulations
- Report Writing
- Investigative Procedures

Initial Assignment

After graduation from the Academy, you are assigned to 45 days of field training, which may be anywhere in California. During this time, you are under the supervision of a field training officer who handles your training and evaluates your progress. If you successfully complete field training, you receive your initial assignment depending on departmental needs.

After one year of service, you receive your California Peace Officer Standards and Training (P.O.S.T.) Basic Certification.

SALARY & BENEFITS

The accompanying chart lists monthly and annual salaries for different ranks within the California Highway Patrol.

Physical Performance Program Incentive

Officers who pass a physical performance program are entitled to incentive pay. Officers with less than 60 months of service receive an additional $65 per pay period and officers with 60 or more months

receive an additional $130 per pay period.

Educational Incentives

Officers who hold an Intermediate Peace Officer Standards and Training (P.O.S.T.) certification or an Associate Degree receive an additional $100 a month. Those with an Advanced P.O.S.T. certification or a Bachelor's Degree receive an additional $200 a month. Sergeants earn an additional 2.5 percent of their base pay for an Intermediate P.O.S.T. certification or an Associate Degree, or 5 percent for an Advanced P.O.S.T. certification or a Bachelor's Degree. (After earning a Basic P.O.S.T. Certificate, officers who meet additional requirements are eligible for an Intermediate or Advanced Certificate. An Intermediate Certificate is awarded to officers with a minimum of two years'

patrol experience and a Bachelor's Degree, or four years' experience and an Associate Degree. Advanced Certificates are earned with a) at least four years' experience and a Master's Degree, b) six years' experience and a Bachelor's Degree, or c) nine years' experience and an Associate Degree. Officers who do not have college degrees may earn these certificates on the basis of training, patrol experience and related education.)

Annual Leave

Vacation and sick time allowances are combined into annual leave. Annual leave is accrued monthly and is determined by how long you have served on the force:

- Up to three years = 19 hours a month

SALARY: AT A GLANCE		
Position	Monthly Salary	Annual Salary
State Traffic Officer Cadet	$2,738 to $3,269	$32,856 to $39,228
State Traffic Officer	$3,156 to $4,478	$37,872 to $53,736
Sergeant	$3,837 to $5,467	$46,044 to $65,604
Lieutenant	$4,856 to $5,343	$58,272 to $64,116
Captain	$5,715 to $6,301	$68,580 to $75,612

Note: Figures supplied by the Department of California Highway Patrol.

- After 10 years = 21 hours a month
- After 15 years = 24 hours a month
- After 25 years = 26 hours a month

You are eligible for annual leave after six months of service.

Holidays

You are granted 12 floating holidays annually.

Uniform and Equipment Allowance

You are initially responsible for the purchase of uniforms. You may receive up to $520 a year for uniform replacement. Motorcycle patrol officers and pilots receive an initial allowance of $255 and $100, respectively, for boots. Necessary safety equipment, including handguns, weather protection, badges, ammunition and handcuffs, is provided by the State.

Bilingual Pay

Bilingual officers who have passed a CHP bilingual proficiency test receive an additional $60 per month at the department's discretion.

Health Coverage

All uniformed officers are offered a choice of comprehensive health plans. You also become eligible for dental coverage after your first year of service.

Retirement

California Highway Patrol Officers must currently retire at age 60. Retirement benefits are 80 percent of the employee's highest annual wage.

APPLICATION - State Traffic Officer Cadet

① COUNTY: mark ONE county nearest to where you wish to take the exam

01 Alameda	11 Glenn	21 Marin	31 Placer	37 San Diego	60 So. Santa Clara:	52 Tehama
02 Alpine	12 Humboldt	22 Mariposa	32 Plumas	38 San Francisco	Gilroy	53 Trinity
03 Amador	13 Imperial	23 Mendocino	33 East Riverside:	39 San Joaquin	44 Santa Cruz	54 Tulare
04 Butte	14 Inyo	24 Merced	Blythe, Indio, Rancho	40 San Luis Obispo	45 Shasta	55 Tuolumne
05 Calaveras	15 Kern	25 Modoc	California, Palm Springs	41 San Mateo	46 Sierra	56 Ventura
06 Colusa	16 Kings	26 Mono	59 West Riverside: Corona,	42 Santa Barbara	47 Siskiyou	57 Yolo
07 Contra Costa	17 Lake	27 Monterey	Riverside, Beaumont, Moreno Valley	43 No. Santa Clara:	48 Solano	58 Yuba
08 Del Norte	18 Lassen	28 Napa	34 Sacramento	Palo Alto, Milpitas,	49 Sonoma	
09 El Dorado	19 Los Angeles	29 Nevada	35 San Benito	Santa Clara, San	50 Stanislaus	
10 Fresno	20 Madera	30 Orange	36 San Bernardino	Jose, Morgan Hill	51 Sutter	

② LAST NAME

(Grid of bubbles A–Z for each letter position)

③ FIRST NAME

(Grid of bubbles A–Z for each letter position)

④ MIDDLE INITIAL

(Column of bubbles A–Z)

⑤ MINIMUM QUALIFICATIONS

ANSWER ALL THREE ITEMS (A, B, C)

A. Are you a high school graduate or the equivalent?   Y   N

B. Have you ever been convicted of a felony?   Y   N

C. Are you a United States citizen?   Y   N

If not, mark the date that you filed for citizenship in Box C: →

BOX C (CITIZENSHIP DATE)

(MONTH / DAY grid of bubbles)

⑥ SOCIAL SECURITY

(Grid of number bubbles 0–9)

⑦ BIRTH DATE

(MONTH / DAY grid of bubbles)

⑧ SEX

Male ☐
Female ☐

⑨ EQUAL EMPLOYMENT OPPORTUNITY

☐ American Indian   ☐ Filipino   ☐ White
☐ Asian   ☐ Hispanic   ☐ Other (specify)
☐ Black   ☐ Pacific Islander   _____

TURN PAGE OVER ➙

CHP 678 (REV.1/94) OPI 038

⑩ STREET NUMBER

⑪ STREET NAME & APARTMENT NUMBER (abbreviate where necessary)

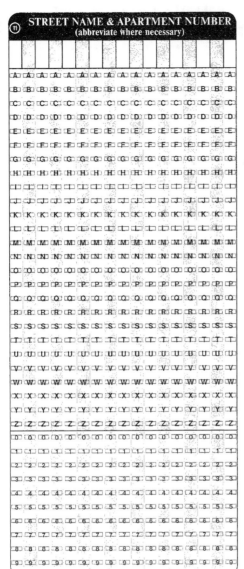

⑫ CITY (abbreviate where necessary)

⑬ STATE

⑭ ZIP CODE

⑮ TELEPHONE #

⑯ CHP-CERTIFIED BILINGUAL SPANISH

If you have already been certified by the CHP, or if you wish to be considered as bilingual or have already been certified as bilingual, blacken the box below.

⑰ RECHECK ALL RESPONSES AND BLACKEN THE BOXES.

⑱ _____

SIGNATURE (use pencil)   DATE

DO NOT FOLD THIS APPLICATION. MAIL THE FORM TO THE CHP USING THE ENCLOSED 9" X 12" PRE-ADDRESSED ENVELOPE.

C · H · A · P · T · E · R

CALIFORNIA STATE POLICE EXAM PLANNER

CHAPTER SUMMARY

This chapter helps you prepare for California's written State Traffic Officer exam by presenting a study plan specially designed for you.

The customized schedules in this chapter are designed to give you a reasonable amount of time to study for the kinds of questions that appear on the State Traffic Officer exam in California, depending on how much time is left before exam day.

After gathering information and conducting a self-evaluation to see how much work you need to do in how much time, you can choose from four customized test preparation schedules. These customized exam planners lead you through practice exams that are based on the real test and chapters that help you sharpen your test-taking skills and knowledge. Whether you have six months to prepare—or just three weeks—here's the way to prepare to score your best.

STEP 1: GET INFORMATION

When: Today   **Time to complete: 1½ hours**

The first thing you need is information. If you haven't already done so, read Chapter 3 to learn about the selection process. Then contact the recruiting office at the phone number listed in Chapter 3. Request a position announcement or exam bulletin and ask when the next exam is scheduled. If no exam is scheduled, ask if you can be put on a mailing list for notification.

Both Chapter 3 and the exam bulletin give an outline of what skills will be tested on the written exam. You can use this information to help you construct your plan in Step 3.

If the exam is scheduled:	do the following self-evaluation and then:
six months or more from now	go to Schedule A
three to six months from now	go to Schedule B
one to three months from now	go to Schedule C
three weeks or less from now	go to Schedule D

STEP 2: SELF-EVALUATION

When: This week   **Time to complete: 4-5 hours**

Find out whether you're ready to take the written exam. First, read Chapter 5, "The Secrets of Test Success." Then take the practice exam in Chapter 6. Score your exam using the answer key at the end. Then match your score with the following analysis.

Score	Analysis
under 60	You need concentrated work in the skills tested. Consider taking classes at the local community college in the areas you're weakest in, or use some of the additional resources listed in Chapters 7–10. After you've spent at least four months working on your skills, retake the test in Chapter 6 and check your score.
61-70	You should spend some time working on your skills. Consider the LearningExpress Skill Builders listed at the back of this book or other books from the library or bookstore. Enlist friends or former teachers to give you some extra help.
70-80	You're in the ballpark. While you only need a score of 70 to pass the real exam, you want to be sure. Work through all the exercises in Chapters 7–10 and then take the second practice test in Chapter 11. If you're score hasn't improved much, try some of the tactics listed above.
80-100	Congratulations! You can pass the real exam, which means you can get to the next steps in the selection process. For insurance, work through the exercises in Chapters 7–10, concentrating on the areas where a little practice will do the most good. Then take the second practice exam in Chapter 11.

STEP 3: MAKE A PLAN

When: This week, after Step 2   Time to complete: 1 hour

There are four sample schedules below, based on the amount of time you have before the exam. If you're the kind of person who needs deadlines and assignments to motivate you for a project, here they are. If you're the kind of person who doesn't like to follow other people's plans, you can use the suggested schedules here to construct your own.

In constructing your plan, you should take into account how much work you need to do. If your score on the practice test wasn't what you had hoped, consider taking some of the steps from Schedule A and getting them into Schedule D somehow, even if you do have only three weeks before the exam.

Even more important than making a plan is making a commitment. You can't improve your skills in reading, writing, and logical reasoning overnight. You have to set aside some time every day for study and practice. Try for at least 20 minutes a day. Twenty minutes daily will do you much more good than two hours on Saturday.

If you have months before the exam, you're lucky. Don't put off your study until the week before the exam! Start now. Even ten minutes a day, with half an hour or more on weekends, can make a big difference in your score—and in your chances of getting the job!

SCHEDULE A: THE LEISURE PLAN

You've already taken the sample test and know that you have at least six months in which to build on your strengths and improve in areas where you're weak. Make the most of your time.

Time	Preparation
Exam minus 6 months	Study the explanations for the practice exam in Chapter 6 until you know you could answer all the questions right. Start going to the library once every two weeks to read books or magazines about law enforcement.
Exam minus 5 months	Read Chapter 7 and work through the exercises. Use at least one of the additional resources listed there. Find other people who are preparing for the test and form a study group.
Exam minus 4 months	Read Chapter 8 and work through the exercises. Use at least one of the additional resources. Start preparing for the rest of the selection process by reading Chapters 12–15.
Exam minus 3 months	Read Chapter 9 and work through the exercises. Use at least one of the additional resources. You're still doing your library reading, aren't you?
Exam minus 2 months	Read Chapter 10 and work through the exercises. Use at least one of the additional resources. Make flash cards of vocabulary and spelling words you come across in your reading.

Exam minus 1 month	Take the practice test in Chapter 11. Use your score to help you decide where to concentrate your efforts this month. Go back to the relevant chapters and use the extra resources listed there, or get the help of a friend or teacher.
Exam minus 1 week	Review both practice tests. See how much you've learned in the past months? Review Chapter 5 and make sure you've taken all the steps to get ready for the exam.
Exam minus 1 day	Relax. Do something unrelated to the exam. Eat a good meal and go to bed at your usual time.

SCHEDULE B: THE JUST-ENOUGH-TIME PLAN

If you have three to six months before the exam, that should be enough time to prepare for the written test, especially if you scored above 60 on the first practice test. This schedule assumes four months; stretch it out or compress it if you have more or less time.

Time	Preparation
Exam minus 4 months	Read Chapter 7 and work through the exercises. Use at least one of the additional resources listed there. Find other people who are preparing for the test and form a study group. Start going to the library once every two weeks to read books about law enforcement.
Exam minus 3 months	Read Chapters 8 and 9 and work through the exercises. Use at least one of the additional resources for each chapter. Keep up your reading program.
Exam minus 2 months	Read Chapter 10 and work through the exercises. Make flash cards of vocabulary and spelling words you come across in your reading.
Exam minus 1 month	Take the practice test in Chapter 11. Use your score to help you decide where to concentrate your efforts this month. Go back to the relevant chapters and use the extra resources listed there, or get the help of a friend or teacher.
Exam minus 1 week	Review both practice tests. See how much you've learned in the past months? Review Chapter 5 and make sure you've taken all the steps to get ready for the exam.
Exam minus 1 day	Relax. Do something unrelated to the exam. Eat a good meal and go to bed at your usual time.

SCHEDULE C: MORE STUDY IN LESS TIME

If you have one to three months before the exam, you still have enough time for some concentrated study that will help you improve your score. This schedule is built around a two-month time frame. If you have only one month, spend an extra couple of hours a week to get all these steps in. If you have three months, take some of the steps from Schedule B and fit them in.

Time	Preparation
Exam minus 8 weeks	Evaluate your performance on the practice test in Chapter 6 to find one or two areas you're weakest in. Choose one or two chapter(s) from among Chapters 7–10 to read in these two weeks. Use some of the additional resources listed there. When you get to those chapters in this plan, review them.
Exam minus 6 weeks	Read Chapters 7 and 8 and work through the exercises.
Exam minus 4 weeks	Read Chapters 9 and 10 and work through the exercises.
Exam minus 2 weeks	Take the second practice test in Chapter 11. Then score it and read the answer explanations until you're sure you understand them. Review the areas where your score is lowest.
Exam minus 1 week	Review Chapters 7–10, concentrating on the areas where a little work can help the most. Review Chapter 5 to make sure you've taken all the steps to get ready for the exam.
Exam minus 1 day	Relax. Do something unrelated to the exam. Eat a good meal and go to bed at your usual time.

SCHEDULE D: THE CRAM PLAN

If you have three weeks or less before the exam, you really have your work cut out for you. Carve half an hour out of your day, *every day*, for study. This schedule assumes you have the whole three weeks to prepare in; if you have less time, you'll have to compress the schedule accordingly.

Time	Preparation
Exam minus 3 weeks	Read Chapters 7 and 8 and work through the exercises.
Exam minus 2 weeks	Read Chapters 9 and 10 and work through the exercises. Take the practice test in Chapter 11.
Exam minus 1 week	Evaluate your performance on the second practice test. Review the parts of Chapters 7–10 that you had the most trouble with. Get a friend or teacher to help you with the section you had the most difficulty with.
Exam minus 2 days	Review both practice tests. Make sure you understand the answer explanations.
Exam minus 1 day	Relax. Do something unrelated to the exam. Eat a good meal and go to bed at your usual time.

STEP 4: SCORE YOUR BEST

When: On Exam Day

If you've followed the plan presented in this chapter, or invented your own based on these guidelines, you *will* score your best—because you're prepared.

THE SECRETS OF TEST SUCCESS

5

CHAPTER SUMMARY

This chapter contains valuable advice for those planning to take a written law enforcement exam: how to prepare, how to beat test anxiety, how to pace yourself as you move through the test, and when to guess. Read this chapter before you take the first sample written exam in this book.

A little preparation goes a long way when it comes to taking a test. If you know about the test beforehand and come prepared physically and mentally, you're already a step ahead. Test preparation reduces your test anxiety, allows you to pace yourself properly on the test, and helps you to do as well as you possibly can. It's a good feeling to walk into a test knowing you've done your best to prepare for it.

FINDING OUT ABOUT THE TEST

The first step is to learn as much as possible about the test you'll be taking. The information you need to know is summarized in the list that follows on the next page.

Must-Know Information

- When and where will the test be given?
- Do I have more than one opportunity to take the test?
- How long will the test take?
- Do most people who take the test finish on time?
- What do I need to bring to the test?

Make sure you know the answers to these questions before you take the test.

Structure and Format of the Test

Find out as much as you can about how the test is organized. Every test is different, but chances are the test you take will be timed and contain mostly multiple-choice questions. Learn as much as you can ahead of time.

- What skills are tested?
- How many sections does the test have?
- How many questions does each section have?
- Are the questions ordered from easy to hard, or is the sequence random?
- How much time is allotted for each section? Are there breaks between sections?
- What is the passing score? How many questions do I have to get right to get that score?
- Will a higher score give me any advantages, like a higher salary or a better rank on the eligibility list? If so, what score would be ideal, yet within reason for me?
- How is the test scored? Is there a penalty for wrong answers? If so, what is it?
- If I finish a section early, can I return to a previous section or move ahead to the next section?
- Can I write in the test booklet, or will I be given scrap paper for my work?

- What should I bring to the test with me? Pencils? Calculator? Ticket of admission? Photo identification? Proof of citizenship?

Some standardized tests are scored in such a way that you are penalized for wrong answers. You *need* this information before you take the test because it will affect how you approach the test. More on that later.

If you complete the *Test Information Sheet* on the next page, you'll be sure to have all the information you need.

COMBATING TEST ANXIETY

Knowing what to expect and being prepared for it is the best defense against test anxiety—that worrisome feeling that keeps you from doing your best. Practice and preparation keep you from succumbing to that feeling.

Nevertheless, even the brightest, most well-prepared test-takers may suffer from occasional bouts of test anxiety. But don't worry—you can overcome it.

Take the Test One Question at a Time

Focus all of your attention on the one question you're answering. Block out any thoughts about questions you've already read or concerns about what's coming next. Concentrate your thinking where it will do the most good—on the question you're answering.

Develop a Positive Attitude

Keep reminding yourself that you're prepared. The fact that you're reading this book means that you're better prepared than most of the others who are taking the test. Remember, it's only a test, and you're going to do your BEST. That's all anyone can ask of you. If that nagging drill sergeant voice inside your head starts send-

TEST INFORMATION SHEET

Must-Know Data

When is the test?_____

Where will it be given?_____

Do you know how to get to the testing site?
- ☐ Yes Make a trial run to see how long it takes to get there at the time of day you'll be making the real trip.
- ☐ No Find out how to get to the testing site and make your trial run.

How long does it take to get to the testing site? _____

What time do you need to leave to get there on time? _____

How long is the test? _____

List the items you need to bring to the test:

_____

_____

Structure and Format of the test

Format: ☐ Multiple-choice ☐ Fill-in-the-blanks
         ☐ True/false ☐ Essay
         ☐ Other

Total # questions: _____

Total # sections: _____

	# Questions	Skills Tested
Section 1		
Section 2		
Section 3		
Section 4		

Passing score:_____   Ideal score:_____

Knowing this information helps you prepare mentally for the test. You'll be able to walk into the test relaxed and confident, knowing you'll do your best.

ing negative messages, combat them with positive ones of your own.

- "I'm doing just fine."
- "I've prepared for this test."
- "I know exactly what to do."
- "I know I can get the score I'm aiming for."

You get the idea. Remember to drown out negative messages with positive ones of your own.

If You Lose Your Concentration

Don't worry about it! It's normal. During a long test it happens to everyone. When your mind is stressed or overexerted, it takes a break whether you want it to or not. It's easy to get your concentration back if you simply acknowledge the fact that you've lost it and take a quick break. You brain needs very little time (seconds really) to rest.

Put your pencil down and close your eyes. Take a few deep breaths and listen to the sound of your breathing. Picture yourself doing something you really enjoy, like playing sports or listening to music. The ten seconds or so that this takes is really all the time your brain needs to relax and get ready to focus again.

Try this technique several times in the days before the test when you feel stressed. The more you practice, the better it will work for you on test day.

If You Freeze

Don't worry about a question that stumps you even though you're sure you know the answer. Mark it and go on to the next question. You can come back to the "stumper" later. Try to put it out of your mind completely until you come back to it. Just let your subconscious mind chew on the question while your conscious mind focuses on the other questions (one at a time, of course). Chances are, the memory block will be gone by the time you return to the question.

If you freeze before you ever begin the test, here's what to do:

1. Take a little time to look over the test.
2. Read a few of the questions.
3. Decide which ones are the easiest and start there.

Before long, you'll be "in the groove."

DURING THE TEST

As you are taking your test, you want to use your time wisely and avoid making errors. Here are a few suggestions for making the most of your time.

TIME MANAGEMENT STRATEGIES
Pace Yourself

The most important time management strategy is pacing yourself. Pacing yourself doesn't just mean how quickly or slowly you can progress through the test. It means knowing how the test is organized, the number of questions you have to get right, and making sure you have enough time to do them. Before you begin a section, take just a few seconds to survey it, noting the number of questions, their organization, and the type of questions that look easier than the rest. Rough out a time schedule based on the time allotted for the section. Mark the halfway point in the section and make a note beside that mark of what time it will be when the testing period is half over.

Keep Moving

Once you begin the test, keep moving! Don't stop to ponder a difficult question. Skip it and move on. Mark the question so you can quickly find it later, if you have time to come back to it. If all questions count the same, then a question that takes you five seconds to answer counts as much as one that takes you several minutes, so pick up the easy points first. Besides, answering the easier questions first helps to build your confidence and gets you in the testing groove. Who knows? As you go through the test, you may even stumble across some relevant information to help you answer those tough questions.

Don't Rush

Keep moving, but don't rush. Think of your mind as a teeter-totter. On one side is your emotional energy. On the other side is your intellectual energy. When your emotional energy is high, your intellectual capacity is low. Remember how difficult it is to reason with someone when you're angry? On the other hand, when your intellectual energy is high, your emotional energy is low.

Rushing raises your emotional energy. Remember the last time you were late for work? All that rushing around causes you to forget important things—like your lunch. Move quickly to keep your mind from wandering, but don't rush and get yourself flustered.

Check Yourself

Check yourself at the halfway mark. If you're a little ahead, you know you're on track and may even have time left to go back and check your work. If you're behind, you have several choices. You can pick up the pace a little, but do this only if you can do it comfortably. Remember—DON'T RUSH! You can also skip around in the remaining portion of the test to pick up as many easy points as possible. This strategy has one drawback, however. If you are marking a score sheet with circles (or "bubbles") and you put the right answers in the wrong bubbles—they're wrong. So pay close attention to the question numbers if you decide to do this.

Set a Target Score

Earlier, you were asked to find out what constituted a passing score and if there was any advantage in earning a higher score. Here's how to use this information to your advantage.

First, let's assume that your only objective is to pass the test because there is no advantage to be gained from a higher score. Figure out how many questions you must answer correctly to pass. *That's how long your test is.* For example, if the test has 100 questions and you need only 70 right to pass, once you're quite sure you've answered 70 questions correctly, you can just breeze through the rest of the test. You'll probably do even better than you did before you hit the passing mark.

Now, let's assume that you need to pass the test, but scoring higher than others who take the test gives you some advantage, a higher placement for example.

In this case, you still want to calculate a passing score. Then set a goal, an ideal score you'd like to earn. Try to make your target score realistic, yet challenging. As you take the test, work first to pass it, then concentrate on earning your target score. This strategy focuses you on the questions you answered correctly, rather than the ones you think are wrong. That way you can build confidence as you go and keep emotional energy to a minimum.

Caution: Don't waste too much time scoring as you go. Just make rough estimates along the way.

AVOIDING ERRORS

When you take the test, you want to make as few errors as possible in the questions you answer. Here are a few tactics to keep in mind.

Control Yourself

Remember the comparison between your mind and a teeter-totter that you read about a few paragraphs ago? Keeping your emotional energy low and your intellectual energy high is the best way to avoid mistakes. If you feel stressed or worried, stop for a few seconds. Acknowledge the feeling (Hmmm! I'm feeling a little pressure here!), take two or three deep breaths, and send yourself a few positive messages. This relieves your emotional anxiety and boosts your intellectual capacity.

Directions

In most testing situations, a proctor reads the instructions aloud before the test begins. Make certain you understand what is expected. If you don't, *ask!* Listen carefully for instructions about how to answer the questions and whether there's a penalty for wrong answers. Make certain you know how much time you have. You may even want to write the amount of time on your test. If you miss this vital information, *ask for it.* You need it to do well on your test.

Answers

This may seem like a silly warning, but it is important. Place your answers in the right blanks or the corresponding bubbles. Right answers in the wrong place earn no points. It's a good idea to check every 5-10 questions, and every time you skip a question, to make sure you're in the right spot. That way you won't need much time to correct your answer sheet if you have made an error.

Choosing the Right Answer by Process of Elimination

As you read a question, you may find it helpful to underline important information or make some notes about what you're reading. When you get to the heart of the question, circle it and make sure you understand what it is asking. If you're not sure of what's being asked, you'll never know whether you've chosen the right answer. What you do next depends on the type of question you're answering.

- If it's math, take a quick look at the answer choices for some clues. Sometimes this helps to put the question in a new perspective and makes it easier to answer. Then make a plan of attack to solve the problem.
- Otherwise, follow this simple *process of elimination* plan to manage your testing time as efficiently as possible: Read each answer choice and make a *quick* decision about what to do with it, marking your test book accordingly:

    The answer seems reasonable; keep it. Put a ✔ next to the answer.
    The answer is awful. Get rid of it. Put an **X** next to the answer.
    You can't make up your mind about the answer, or you don't understand it. Keep it for now. Put a **?** next to it.

Whatever you do, don't waste time dilly-dallying over each answer choice. If you can't figure out what an answer choice means, don't worry about it. If it's the right answer, you'll probably be able to eliminate all the others, and, if it's the wrong answer, another answer will probably strike you more obviously as the right answer.

If you haven't eliminated any answers at all, skip the question temporarily, but don't forget to mark the question so you can come back to it later if you have time. If the test has no penalty for wrong answers, and you're certain that you could never answer this question in a million years, pick an answer and move on!

If you've eliminated all but one answer, just reread the circled part of the question to make sure you're answering exactly what's asked. Mark your answer sheet and move on to the next question.

Here's what to do when you've eliminated some, but not all of the answer choices. Compare the remaining answers looking for similarities and differences, reasoning your way through these choices. Try to eliminate those choices that don't seem as strong to you. But DON'T eliminate an answer just because you don't understand it. You may even be able to use relevant information from other parts of the test. If you've narrowed it down to a single answer, check it against the circled question to be sure you've answered it. Then mark your answer sheet and move on. If you're down to only two or three answer choices, you've improved your odds of getting the question right. Make an *educated* guess and move on. However, if you think you can do better with more time, mark the question as one to return to later.

If You're Penalized for Wrong Answers

You *must know* whether you'll be penalized for wrong answers before you begin the test. If you don't, ask the proctor before the test begins. Whether you make a guess or not depends upon the penalty. Some standardized tests are scored in such a way that every wrong answer reduces your score by a fraction of a point, and these can really add up against you! Whatever the penalty, if you can eliminate enough choices to make the odds of answering the question better than the penalty for getting it wrong, make a guess. This is called *educated guessing.*

Let's imagine you are taking a test in which each answer has five choices and you are penalized ¼ of a point for each wrong answer. If you cannot eliminate any of the answer choices, you're better off leaving the answer blank because the odds of guessing correctly are one in five. However, if you can eliminate two of the choices as definitely wrong, the odds are now in your favor. You have a one in three chance of answering the question correctly. Fortunately, few tests are scored using such elaborate means, but if your test is one of them, know the penalties and calculate your odds before you take a guess on a question.

If You Finish Early

Use any time you have left to do the following:

- Go back to questions you marked to return to and try them again.
- Check your work on all the other questions. If you have a good reason for thinking a response is wrong, change it.
- Review your answer sheet. Make sure that you've put the answers in the right places and that you've marked only one answer for each question. (Most tests are scored in such a way that questions with more than one answer are marked wrong.)
- If you've erased an answer, make sure you've done a good job of it.
- Check for stray marks on your answer sheet that could distort your score.

Whatever you do, don't just take a nap when you've finished a test section. Make every second count by checking your work over and over again until time is called.

THE DAYS BEFORE THE TEST

Physical Activity

Get some exercise in the days preceding the test. You'll send some extra oxygen to your brain and allow your thinking performance to peak on test day. Moderation is the key here. Don't exercise so much that you feel exhausted, but a little physical activity will invigorate your body and brain.

Balanced Diet

Like your body, your brain needs the proper nutrients to function well. Eat plenty of fruits and vegetables in the days before the test. Foods that are high in lecithin, such as fish and beans, are especially good choices. Lecithin is a mineral your brain needs for peak performance. You may even consider a visit to your local pharmacy to buy a bottle of lecithin tablets several weeks before your test.

Rest

Get plenty of sleep the nights before you take the test. Don't overdo it, though, or you'll make yourself as groggy as if you were overtired. Go to bed at a reasonable time, early enough to get the number of hours you need to function effectively. You'll feel relaxed and rested if you've gotten plenty of sleep in the days before you take the test.

Trial Run

At some point before you take the test, make a trial run to the testing center to see how long it takes to get there. Rushing raises your emotional energy and lowers your intellectual capacity, so you want to allow plenty of time on test day to get to the testing center. Arriving 10–15 minutes early gives you time to relax and get situated.

The Night Before

Get ready all those things you need to bring with you to the test, such as pencils, identification, admission ticket, etc. Make sure you have at least three pencils, including one with a dull point for faster gridding of a bubble answer sheet. You don't want to waste time the morning of the test hunting around for these things.

TEST DAY

It's finally here, the day of the big test. Set your alarm early enough to allow plenty of time. Eat a good breakfast. Avoid anything that's really high in sugar, such as donuts. A sugar high turns into a sugar low after an hour or so. Cereal and toast or anything with complex carbohydrates is a good choice. Eat only moderate amounts. You don't want to take a test feeling stuffed!

Dress in layers. You can never tell what the conditions will be like in the testing room. Your proctor just might be a member of the polar bear club.

Pack a high energy snack to take with you. You might get a break sometime during the test when you can grab a quick snack. Bananas are great. They have a moderate amount of sugar and plenty of brain nutri-

ents, such as potassium. Most proctors won't allow you to eat a snack while you're testing, but a peppermint shouldn't pose a problem. Peppermints are like smelling salts for your brain. If you lose your concentration or suffer from a momentary mental block, a peppermint can get you back on track.

Leave early enough so you have plenty of time to get to the test center. Allow a few minutes for unexpected traffic. When you arrive, locate the restroom and use it. Few things interfere with concentration as much as a full bladder. Then check in, find your seat, and make sure it's comfortable. If it isn't, tell the proctor and ask to change to a location you find more suitable.

Now relax and think positively! Before you know it the test will be over, and you'll walk away knowing you've done the best you can.

AFTER THE TEST

Two things:

1. Plan a little celebration.
2. Go to it.

If you have something to look forward to after the test is over, you may find it easier to prepare well for the test and to keep moving during the test.

GOOD LUCK!

C·H·A·P·T·E·R 6
CALIFORNIA STATE POLICE EXAM 1

CHAPTER SUMMARY

This is the first of two exams in this book based on the entry-level law enforcement tests of the California Peace Officer Standards and Training (POST) Commission, which the California Highway Patrol uses as its written exam. You can use this test to see how you would do if you had to take the test today.

T he test that follows is modeled on the California POST Commission's reading and writing exam for entry-level law enforcement personnel. This test is used to assess applicants for the position of State Traffic Officer for the California Highway Patrol.

There are 105 questions on this test, 65 in Book One and 40 in Book Two. Book One covers clarity of expression (grammar), vocabulary, spelling, and reading comprehension. Book Two is a different kind of reading test where you have to fill in the missing words in a passage. The directions for each kind of question are included in the test. The answer sheet you should use to mark your answers comes before the test, and the answer key and an explanation of how to score your test results come after.

One of the keys to doing well on any exam is simply knowing what to expect. While there's no substitute for having the skills the exam is testing for, the experience of taking similar exams goes a long way toward enhancing your self-confidence—and self-confidence is key to doing well.

Use this test to get a benchmark: Where are you starting as you begin your preparation for the exam? On the real test you'll have two and a half hours to answer all the questions, but, for now, don't worry about timing. Just take the test in as relaxed a manner as you can. Make sure you have enough time, however, to do the whole test at a sitting. Find a quiet spot where you won't be interrupted, and turn off the radio and TV. When you've finished, turn to the answer key to see how you did.

BOOK ONE

1.	(a)	(b)	(c)	(d)	23.	(a)	(b)	(c)	(d)	45.	(a)	(b)	(c)	(d)
2.	(a)	(b)	(c)	(d)	24.	(a)	(b)	(c)	(d)	46.	(a)	(b)	(c)	(d)
3.	(a)	(b)	(c)	(d)	25.	(a)	(b)	(c)	(d)	47.	(a)	(b)	(c)	(d)
4.	(a)	(b)	(c)	(d)	26.	(a)	(b)	(c)	(d)	48.	(a)	(b)	(c)	(d)
5.	(a)	(b)	(c)	(d)	27.	(a)	(b)	(c)	(d)	49.	(a)	(b)	(c)	(d)
6.	(a)	(b)	(c)	(d)	28.	(a)	(b)	(c)	(d)	50.	(a)	(b)	(c)	(d)
7.	(a)	(b)	(c)	(d)	29.	(a)	(b)	(c)	(d)	51.	(a)	(b)	(c)	(d)
8.	(a)	(b)	(c)	(d)	30.	(a)	(b)	(c)	(d)	52.	(a)	(b)	(c)	(d)
9.	(a)	(b)	(c)	(d)	31.	(a)	(b)	(c)	(d)	53.	(a)	(b)	(c)	(d)
10.	(a)	(b)	(c)	(d)	32.	(a)	(b)	(c)	(d)	54.	(a)	(b)	(c)	(d)
11.	(a)	(b)	(c)	(d)	33.	(a)	(b)	(c)	(d)	55.	(a)	(b)	(c)	(d)
12.	(a)	(b)	(c)	(d)	34.	(a)	(b)	(c)	(d)	56.	(a)	(b)	(c)	(d)
13.	(a)	(b)	(c)	(d)	35.	(a)	(b)	(c)	(d)	57.	(a)	(b)	(c)	(d)
14.	(a)	(b)	(c)	(d)	36.	(a)	(b)	(c)	(d)	58.	(a)	(b)	(c)	(d)
15.	(a)	(b)	(c)	(d)	37.	(a)	(b)	(c)	(d)	59.	(a)	(b)	(c)	(d)
16.	(a)	(b)	(c)	(d)	38.	(a)	(b)	(c)	(d)	60.	(a)	(b)	(c)	(d)
17.	(a)	(b)	(c)	(d)	39.	(a)	(b)	(c)	(d)	61.	(a)	(b)	(c)	(d)
18.	(a)	(b)	(c)	(d)	40.	(a)	(b)	(c)	(d)	62.	(a)	(b)	(c)	(d)
19.	(a)	(b)	(c)	(d)	41.	(a)	(b)	(c)	(d)	63.	(a)	(b)	(c)	(d)
20.	(a)	(b)	(c)	(d)	42.	(a)	(b)	(c)	(d)	64.	(a)	(b)	(c)	(d)
21.	(a)	(b)	(c)	(d)	43.	(a)	(b)	(c)	(d)	65.	(a)	(b)	(c)	(d)
22.	(a)	(b)	(c)	(d)	44.	(a)	(b)	(c)	(d)					

BOOK TWO

WRITE 1ST LETTER OF WORD HERE

CODE LETTERS HERE

1	2	3	4	5	6	7	8	9	10

A A A A A A A A A A
B B B B B B B B B B
C C C C C C C C C C
D D D D D D D D D D
E E E E E E E E E E
F F F F F F F F F F
G G G G G G G G G G
H H H H H H H H H H
I I I I I I I I I I
J J J J J J J J J J
K K K K K K K K K K
L L L L L L L L L L
M M M M M M M M M M
N N N N N N N N N N
O O O O O O O O O O
P P P P P P P P P P
Q Q Q Q Q Q Q Q Q Q
R R R R R R R R R R
S S S S S S S S S S
T T T T T T T T T T
U U U U U U U U U U
V V V V V V V V V V
W W W W W W W W W W
X X X X X X X X X X
Y Y Y Y Y Y Y Y Y Y
Z Z Z Z Z Z Z Z Z Z

11	12	13	14	15	16	17	18	19	20

A A A A A A A A A A
B B B B B B B B B B
C C C C C C C C C C
D D D D D D D D D D
E E E E E E E E E E
F F F F F F F F F F
G G G G G G G G G G
H H H H H H H H H H
I I I I I I I I I I
J J J J J J J J J J
K K K K K K K K K K
L L L L L L L L L L
M M M M M M M M M M
N N N N N N N N N N
O O O O O O O O O O
P P P P P P P P P P
Q Q Q Q Q Q Q Q Q Q
R R R R R R R R R R
S S S S S S S S S S
T T T T T T T T T T
U U U U U U U U U U
V V V V V V V V V V
W W W W W W W W W W
X X X X X X X X X X
Y Y Y Y Y Y Y Y Y Y
Z Z Z Z Z Z Z Z Z Z

21	22	23	24	25	26	27	28	29	30

A A A A A A A A A A
B B B B B B B B B B
C C C C C C C C C C
D D D D D D D D D D
E E E E E E E E E E
F F F F F F F F F F
G G G G G G G G G G
H H H H H H H H H H
I I I I I I I I I I
J J J J J J J J J J
K K K K K K K K K K
L L L L L L L L L L
M M M M M M M M M M
N N N N N N N N N N
O O O O O O O O O O
P P P P P P P P P P
Q Q Q Q Q Q Q Q Q Q
R R R R R R R R R R
S S S S S S S S S S
T T T T T T T T T T
U U U U U U U U U U
V V V V V V V V V V
W W W W W W W W W W
X X X X X X X X X X
Y Y Y Y Y Y Y Y Y Y
Z Z Z Z Z Z Z Z Z Z

31	32	33	34	35	36	37	38	39	40

A A A A A A A A A A
B B B B B B B B B B
C C C C C C C C C C
D D D D D D D D D D
E E E E E E E E E E
F F F F F F F F F F
G G G G G G G G G G
H H H H H H H H H H
I I I I I I I I I I
J J J J J J J J J J
K K K K K K K K K K
L L L L L L L L L L
M M M M M M M M M M
N N N N N N N N N N
O O O O O O O O O O
P P P P P P P P P P
Q Q Q Q Q Q Q Q Q Q
R R R R R R R R R R
S S S S S S S S S S
T T T T T T T T T T
U U U U U U U U U U
V V V V V V V V V V
W W W W W W W W W W
X X X X X X X X X X
Y Y Y Y Y Y Y Y Y Y
Z Z Z Z Z Z Z Z Z Z

CALIFORNIA STATE POLICE EXAM 1 BOOK 1

PART ONE: CLARITY

In the following sets of sentences, choose the sentence that is most clearly written.

1.
a. Because Officer Alvarez had a warrant, she was able to search the suspect's car, where she found $200,000 worth of cocaine.
b. Officer Alvarez was able to search the suspect's car, where she found $200,000 worth of cocaine. Because she had a warrant.
c. $200,000 worth of cocaine was found. The result of a search by Office Alvarez of the suspect's car, because she had a warrant.
d. Because of a warrant and a search of the suspect's car. $200,000 worth of cocaine was found by Officer Alvarez.

2.
a. The guard, like the prisoners, were sick of the food in the prison mess hall, and yesterday he went to the warden and complained.
b. The guard, like the prisoners, was sick of the food in the prison mess hall, and yesterday he goes to the warden and complains.
c. The guard, like the prisoners, was sick of the food in the prison mess hall, and yesterday he went to the warden and complained.
d. The guard, like the prisoners, were sick of the food in the prison mess hall, and yesterday he goes to the warden and complained.

3.
a. Lieutenant Wells did not think the prisoner could be capable to escape.
b. Lieutenant Wells did not think that the prisoner capable of escaping.
c. Lieutenant Wells did not think the prisoner capable of escape.
d. Lieutenant Wells did not think that the prisoner capable to escape.

4.
a. The masked gunman ordered the bank customers to remove their jewelry and lie down on the floor, with a growl.
b. The masked gunman ordered the bank customers to remove their jewelry, with a growl, and lie down on the floor.
c. The masked gunman ordered the bank customers with a growl. To remove their jewelry and lie down on the floor.
d. With a growl, the masked gunman ordered the bank customers to remove their jewelry and lie down on the floor.

5.
a. Of all the dogs in the K-9 Corps, Zelda is the most bravest.
b. Of all the dogs in the K-9 Corps, Zelda is the bravest.
c. Of all the dogs in the K-9 Corps, Zelda is the braver.
d. Of all the dogs in the K-9 Corps, Zelda is the more brave.

6.

a. My partner Rosie and I, we did not like each other at first, but now we get along fine.

b. My partner Rosie and I did not like each other at first, but now her and I get along fine.

c. My partner Rosie and me did not like each other at first, but now she and I get along fine.

d. My partner Rosie and I did not like each other at first, but now we get along fine.

7.

a. A sharpshooter for many years, Miles Johnson could shoot a pea off a person's shoulder from 70 yards away.

b. Miles Johnson could shoot a pea off a person's shoulder from 70 yards away, a sharpshooter for many years.

c. A sharpshooter for many years, a pea could be shot off a person's shoulder by Miles Johnson from 70 yards away.

d. From 70 yards away, a sharpshooter for many years, Miles Johnson could shoot a pea off a person's shoulder.

8.

a. The TV show *Colombo* is said to have been inspired in part of the classic Russian novel *Crime and Punishment.*

b. The TV show *Colombo* is said to have been inspired in part by the classic Russian novel *Crime and Punishment.*

c. The TV show *Colombo* is said to have been inspired in part off of the classic Russian novel *Crime and Punishment*

d. The TV show *Colombo* is said to have been inspired in part from the classic Russian novel *Crime and Punishment.*

9.

a. Recession, as well as budget cuts, is hard on the cop on the beat.

b. Recession and budget cuts is hard on the cop on the beat.

c. Recession, as well as budget cuts, are hard on the cop on the beat.

d. Budget cuts, as well as the recession, is hard on the cop on the beat.

10.

a. For three weeks the Merryville Fire Chief received taunting calls from an arsonist, who would not say where he intended to set the next fire.

b. The Merryville Fire Chief received taunting calls from an arsonist, but he would not say where he intended to set the next fire, for three weeks.

c. He would not say where he intended to set the next fire, but for three weeks the Merryville Fire Chief received taunting calls from an arsonist.

d. The Merryville Police Chief received taunting calls from an arsonist for three weeks, not saying where he intended to set the next fire.

11.

a. Some people say jury duty is a nuisance that just takes up their precious time and that we don't get paid enough.

b. Some people say jury duty is a nuisance that just takes up your precious time and that one doesn't get paid enough.

c. Some people say jury duty is a nuisance that just takes up one's precious time and that one doesn't get paid enough.

d. Some people say jury duty is a nuisance that just takes up our precious time and that they don't get paid enough.

12.

a. Kate Meyers and several other officers has recently received a well-deserved promotion.

b. Several officers, including Kate Meyers, has recently received a well-deserved promotion.

c. Kate Meyers, along with several other officers, have recently received well-deserved promotions.

d. Several officers, including Kate Meyers, have recently received well-deserved promotions.

13.

a. Doctor Falkenrath believes that neither immorality nor amorality is a spiritual defect.

b. Doctor Falkenrath believes that neither immorality nor amorality are a spiritual defect.

c. Doctor Falkenrath believes that immorality and amorality are not a spiritual defect.

d. Doctor Falkenrath believes that both immorality and amorality is not spiritual defects.

14.

a. An abused woman's cries for help were sometimes ignored, and she is advised to go back to her abuser.

b. An abused woman's cries for help were sometimes ignored, and she will be advised to go back to her abuser.

c. An abused woman's cries for help are sometimes ignored, and she is advised to go back to her abuser.

d. An abused woman's cries for help are sometimes ignored, and she was advised to go back to her abuser.

15.

a. Sergeant Ahlamady often bought pizza for herself and I.

b. Sergeant Ahlamady often bought pizza for herself and me.

c. Sergeant Ahlamady often bought pizza for her and me.

d. Sergeant Ahlamady often bought pizza for herself and myself.

PART TWO: VOCABULARY

In each of the following sentences, choose the word or phrase that most nearly expresses the same meaning as the underlined word.

16. The officer was an <u>indispensable</u> member of the department.
    a. determined
    b. experienced
    c. essential
    d. creative

17. The attorney wanted to <u>expedite</u> the process.
    a. accelerate
    b. evaluate
    c. reverse
    d. justify

18. The suspect gave a <u>plausible</u> explanation for his presence at the scene.
    a. unbelievable
    b. insufficient
    c. apologetic
    d. credible

19. He based his conclusion on what he <u>inferred</u> from the evidence, not on what he actually observed.
    a. intuited
    b. imagined
    c. surmised
    d. implied

20. The neighborhood watch group presented its <u>ultimatum</u> to the drug dealers.
    a. earnest plea
    b. formal petition
    c. solemn promise
    d. non-negotiable demand

21. The county coroner's examination of the body was <u>meticulous</u>.
    a. delicate
    b. painstaking
    c. responsible
    d. objective

22. The police spokesperson must <u>articulate</u> the philosophy of an entire department.
    a. trust
    b. refine
    c. verify
    d. express

23. Different methods to <u>alleviate</u> the situation were debated.
    a. ease
    b. tolerate
    c. clarify
    d. intensify

24. The matter reached its conclusion only after <u>diplomatic</u> efforts by both sides.
    a. tactful
    b. delaying
    c. elaborate
    d. combative

25. Although the neighborhood was said to be safe, they heard <u>intermittent</u> gunfire all night long.
  a. protracted
  b. periodic
  c. disquieting
  d. vehement

26. As soon as the details of the robbery were released to the media, the police department was <u>inundated</u> with calls from people who said they had seen the mysterious blue van.
  a. provided
  b. bothered
  c. rewarded
  d. flooded

27. Regarding the need for more police protection in City Park, the group's opinion was <u>unanimous</u>.
  a. divided
  b. uniform
  c. adamant
  d. clear-cut

28. The City Council has given <u>tentative</u> approval to the idea of banning smoking from all public buildings.
  a. provisional
  b. ambiguous
  c. wholehearted
  d. unnecessary

29. Most members of the community thought the Neighborhood Guards' red hats were <u>ostentatious</u>.
  a. hilarious
  b. pretentious
  c. outrageous
  d. obnoxious

30. The <u>prerequisite</u> training for this exercise is an advanced firearms course.
  a. required
  b. optional
  c. preferred
  d. advisable

PART THREE: SPELLING

In each of the following sentences, choose the correct spelling of the missing word.

31. It was a _____ day for the Fire Fighters' annual picnic.
  a. superb
  b. supperb
  c. supurb
  d. sepurb

32. The first time Officer Lin drove the squad car into town, all his old friends were _____.
  a. jellous
  b. jealous
  c. jealuse
  d. jeolous

33. When we were halfway up the hill, we heard a
_____ explosion.
   a. teriffic
   b. terrific
   c. terriffic
   d. terific

34. If elected, my brother Roy will make a fine
_____.
   a. sherrif
   b. sherriff
   c. sherif
   d. sheriff

35. Catching the persons responsible for the fire
has become an _____ for Officer Beatty.
   a. obssession
   b. obsessian
   c. obsession
   d. obsessiun

36. Officer Alvarez would have fired her weapon,
but she did not want to place the hostage in
_____.
   a. jeoperdy
   b. jepardy
   c. jeapardy
   d. jeopardy

37. Because of the danger they were in, the soldiers were unable to enjoy the _____
scenery.
   a. magniffisent
   b. magnifisent
   c. magnificent
   d. magnifficent

38. From inside the box came a strange
_____ whirring sound.
   a. mechinical
   b. mechanical
   c. mechenical
   d. machanical

39. The community was shocked when Cindy
Pierce, the president of the senior class, was
arrested for selling _____ drugs.
   a. elicitt
   b. ellicit
   c. illicet
   d. illicit

40. There will be an immediate _____ into
the mayor's death.
   a. inquiry
   b. inquirry
   c. enquirry
   d. enquery

41. Al Guggins was thrown into the East River
after he attempted to _____ his contract
with the mob.
   a. termanate
   b. termenate
   c. terrminate
   d. terminate

42. Ben Alshieka feels that he is being
_____ for his religious beliefs.
   a. persecuted
   b. pursecuted
   c. presecuted
   d. perrsecuted

43. What on earth is that _____ odor?
   a. peculior
   b. peculiar
   c. peculliar
   d. puculior

44. Some people say that _____ is not a true science.
   a. psycology
   b. pyschology
   c. psychollogy
   d. psychology

45. Ronald Pinkington was twenty-seven years old before he got his driver's _____.
   a. lisense
   b. lisence
   c. lycence
   d. license

PART FOUR: READING COMPREHENSION

Several reading passages, each accompanied by three or more questions, follow. Answer each question based on what is stated or implied in the preceding passage.

Most criminals do not suffer from anti-social personality disorder; however, nearly all persons with this disorder have been in trouble with the law. Sometimes labeled "sociopaths," they are a grim problem for society. Their crimes range from con games to murder, and they are set apart by what appears to be a complete lack of conscience. Often attractive and charming, and always inordinately self-confident, they nevertheless demonstrate a disturbing emotional shallowness, as if they had been born without a faculty as vital as sight or hearing. These individuals are not legally insane, nor do they suffer from the distortions of thought associated with mental illness; however, some experts believe they are mentally ill. If so, it is an illness that is exceptionally resistant to treatment, particularly since these individuals have a marked inability to learn from the past. It is this latter trait that makes them a special problem for law enforcement officials. Their ability to mimic true emotion enables them to convince prison officials, judges, and psychiatrists that they feel remorse. When released from incarceration, however, they go back to their old tricks, to their con games, their impulsive destructiveness, and their sometimes lethal deceptions.

46. Based on the passage, which of the following is likely NOT a characteristic of the person with anti-social personality disorder?
   a. delusions of persecution
   b. feelings of superiority
   c. inability to suffer deeply
   d. inability to feel joy

47. Which of the following careers would probably best suit the person with an anti-social personality?
   a. soldier with ambition to make officer
   b. warden of a large penitentiary
   c. loan officer in a bank
   d. salesperson dealing in non-existent real estate

48. Based on the passage, which of the following words best sums up the inner emotional life of the person with an anti-social personality?
   a. angry
   b. empty
   c. anxious
   d. repressed

49. According to the passage, which of the following characteristics is most helpful to the person with an anti-social personality in getting out of trouble with the law?
  a. inability to learn from the past
  b. ability to mimic the emotions of others
  c. attractiveness and charm
  d. indifference to the suffering of others

Hearsay evidence, which is the secondhand reporting of a statement, is allowed in court only when the truth of the statement is irrelevant. Hearsay that depends on the statement's truthfulness is inadmissible because the witness does not appear in court and swear an oath to tell the truth, his or her demeanor when making the statement is not visible to the jury, the accuracy of the statement cannot be tested under cross-examination, and to introduce it would be to deprive the accused of the constitutional right to confront the accuser. Hearsay is admissible, however, when the truth of the statement is unimportant. If, for example, a defendant claims to have been unconscious at a certain time, and a witness claims that the defendant actually spoke to her at that time, this evidence would be admissible because the truth of what the defendant actually said is irrelevant.

50. The main purpose of the passage is to
  a. explain why hearsay evidence abridges the rights of the accused
  b. question the truth of hearsay evidence
  c. argue that rules about the admissibility of hearsay evidence should be changed.
  d. specify which use of hearsay evidence is inadmissible and why

51. Which of the following is NOT a reason given in the passage for the inadmissibility of hearsay evidence?
  a. Rumors are not necessarily credible.
  b. The person making the original statement was not under oath.
  c. The jury should be able to watch the gestures and facial expressions of the person making the statement.
  d. The person making the statement cannot be cross-examined.

52. How does the passage explain the proper use of hearsay evidence?
  a. by listing a set of criteria
  b. by providing a hypothetical example
  c. by referring to the Constitution
  d. by citing case law

Police officers are held to a higher standard of conduct than most citizens. Should an officer behave in a disruptive manner, make an offensive joke, or behave in an otherwise uncivil manner, even while off duty, community leaders, public officials, and the media react not only with disapprobation and censure, but even with surprise. Police officers are expected to be idealists. One often hears the expression "jaded cop," but when is a corporate executive ever disparaged as a "jaded businessman?" A businessman whose moral sense has been fatigued or one who lacks compassion is not considered notable, yet a police officer is expected to have high ideals even though he or she confronts human nature at its most disillusioning every day.

This is as it should be. As police officers are the keepers of civil order, they must exemplify civil behavior. Civil order depends less upon legal coercion than upon mutual respect and common ideals. Committed to the ideals of justice and truth, police officers must practice fairness and accuracy, even in their speech. Sworn to uphold individual rights, they must treat every individual with respect. A high standard of civil conduct is not merely a matter of community relations, but speaks to the essence of a police officer's role. By the same token, the public should treat police officers with the respect due those who must adhere to a higher standard of tolerance, understanding, moderation, and civility, even while working under extraordinarily trying conditions.

53. Which of the following best expresses the main idea of the passage?
a. High standards should apply to businessmen as well as to police officers.
b. Police officers are held to unrealistic standards of behavior.
c. Police officers must remain idealistic, despite the disillusioning nature of their work.
d. A police officer should uphold common ideals, both as expressed in law and as required to keep the peace.

54. The passage suggests that police officers should refrain from racial slurs for all of the following reasons EXCEPT
a. as generalizations, such slurs are unfair and inaccurate
b. such slurs are disrespectful to individuals
c. such slurs harm the relationship between the community and the police
d. such slurs are hurtful to the morale of a multiracial police force

55. According to the passage, a police officer should be held to a different standard than a businessman because
a. a police officer's very job is concerned with civil behavior
b. police officers are more jaded
c. police officers are expected to be honest
d. a police officer is a figure of civil authority

56. Why does civil conduct "speak to the very essence of a police officer's role?"
a. because a police officer is a public servant
b. because a police officer who behaves in an uncivil manner meets with public censure
c. because civil conduct is necessary in order to keep the civil peace
d. because a police officer upholds the law

57. Which of the following is NOT mentioned in the passage as a quality a police officer must exemplify?
a. politeness
b. courage
c. justice
d. moderation

Adolescents are at high risk for violent crime. Although they make up only 14 percent of the population age 12 and over, 30 percent of all violent crimes—1.9 million—were committed against them. Because crimes against adolescents are likely to be committed by offenders of the same age (as well as same sex and race), preventing violence among and against adolescents is a twofold challenge. Adolescents are at risk of being both victims and perpetrators of violence. New violence-prevention programs in urban middle schools help reduce the crime rate by teaching both victims and perpetrators of such violence the skills of conflict resolution and how to apply reason to disputes, as well as by changing attitudes towards achieving respect through violence and towards the need to retaliate. These programs provide a safe place for students to discuss their conflicts and therefore prove appealing to students at risk.

58. What is the main idea of the passage?
  a. Adolescents are more likely to commit crimes than older people and must therefore be taught nonviolence in order to protect society.
  b. Middle school students appreciate the conflict resolution skills they acquire in violence-prevention programs.
  c. Middle school violence-prevention programs are designed to help to lower the rate of crimes against adolescents.
  d. Violence against adolescents is increasing.

59. Which of the following is NOT mentioned in the passage as a skill taught by middle school violence-prevention programs?
  a. being reasonable in emotional situations
  b. settling disputes without violence
  c. avoiding the need for vengeance
  d. keeping one's temper

60. According to the passage, which of the following statements about adolescents is true?
  a. Adolescents are disproportionately likely to be victims of violent crime.
  b. Adolescents are more likely to commit violent crimes than other segments of the population.
  c. Adolescents are the victims of 14% of the nation's violent crimes.
  d. Adolescents are reluctant to attend violence-prevention programs.

61. According to the passage, why is preventing violence against adolescents a "twofold challenge"?
  a. because adolescents are twice as likely to be victims of violent crime as members of other age groups
  b. because adolescents must change both their violent behavior and their attitudes towards violence
  c. because adolescents must be prevented from both perpetrating and being victimized by violent crime
  d. because adolescents are vulnerable yet reluctant to listen to adult advice

Evidence concerning the character of a witness must be limited to questions of truthfulness. The credibility of a witness can be attacked by any party, and by evidence of a prior conviction for a felony, so long as the relevance of the conviction to the question of truthfulness is deemed by the court to outweigh the prejudicial damage caused to the witness. If, for example, the witness is guilty of some crime which the jury might find repugnant but which is not relevant to the witness's credibility, this would be deemed unacceptably prejudicial. The elements of credibility which can be impeached are perception, memory, clarity, and sincerity. Police officers should not base an arrest on the testimony of an untruthful or otherwise unreliable witness—a witness who is mentally unstable, senile, or intoxicated, for example. Officers should recognize that a case based on the testimony of a witness with prior felony convictions is vulnerable to dismissal.

62. What is the primary purpose of the passage?
   a. to review the criteria for impeaching the credibility of a witness
   b. to argue for the importance of determining the credibility of a witness before arresting a suspect
   c. to raise questions concerning the reliability of witnesses with prior convictions
   d. to teach police officers proper witness interrogation techniques

63. Which of the following would not be admissible to impeach the credibility of a witness?
   a. proof of a felony conviction
   b. a psychiatric evaluation
   c. a neighbor's claim that the witness is a liar
   d. a claim that the witness is prone to spousal abuse

64. According to the passage, why shouldn't the police base their case on the testimony of an untruthful witness?
   a. The accused might be innocent.
   b. The case might be dismissed.
   c. The police will be embarrassed in court.
   d. The police will be vulnerable to a lawsuit.

65. Which of the following witnesses would be least likely to be vulnerable to having their credibility impeached, according to the criteria set forth in the passage?
   a. a nearsighted person who wasn't wearing glasses
   b. an alcoholic
   c. a petty thief
   d. a person with a psychiatric history

BOOK TWO

This is a test of your reading ability. In the following passages, words have been omitted. Each numbered set of dashed blank lines indicates where a word is left out; each dash represents one letter of the missing word. The correct word should not only make sense in the sentence but also have the number of letters indicated by the dashes.

Read through the whole passage, and then begin filling in the missing words. Fill in as many missing words as possible. If you aren't sure of the answer, take a guess.

Then mark your answers on the answer sheet as follows: Write the **first letter** of the word you have chosen in the square under the number of the word. Then blacken the circle of that letter of the alphabet under the square.

Only the blackened alphabet circles will be scored. The words you write on this page and the letters you write at the top of the column on the answer sheet **will not be scored.** Make sure that you blacken the appropriate circle in each column.

Many people become angry when they hear that prison inmates have the opportunity to study for their 1) _ _ _ _ school equivalency diplomas, take college courses, and even earn 2) _ _ _ _ _ _ _ degrees while they are serving 3) _ _ _ _. Such educational services are often provided at 4) _ _ charge to the inmates, which means that the 5) _ _ _ _ _ are borne by taxpayers. Many people see these 6) _ _ _ _ educational services as coddling criminals, and providing "rewards" for lawbreakers. Higher education is 7) _ _ _ _ _ _ _ _ _ and it is frustrating to many people to see convicted criminals 8) _ _ _ for free what working people have to struggle so hard to 9) _ _ _ _ _ _ _ for their children. On the other hand, those 10) _ _ _ support educational services for inmates argue that it is in society's 11) _ _ _ _ interest to provide such services. Rather 12) _ _ _ _ being seen as a reward for 13) _ _ _ _ _ _ _ _ _ _ _ _, education should be viewed as an investment in social order. A decent 14) _ _ _ _ _ _ _ _ _ will make the ex-offender 15) _ _ _ _ employable, and that, in turn, should remove one 16) _ _ _ _ _ _ for repeat offenses—the inability to earn a living in a socially acceptable 17) _ _ _. We should not 18) _ _ _ _ educational opportunities to those in 19) _ _ _ _ _ _ if we expect them to become useful citizens when 20) _ _ _ _ leave.

(continued on page 17)

Members for high-risk occupations like law enforcement and fire fighting form tightly knit groups. The dangers they share naturally **21)** _ _ _ _ them close, as does the knowledge that their **22)** _ _ _ _ _ are sometimes in one another's hands. The bonds of loyalty and trust help police **23)** _ _ _ _ _ _ _ _ work more effectively. However, the sense **24)** _ _ loyalty can be taken to **25)** _ _ _ _ _ _ _ _. Sometimes officers believe that they always must defend their comrades' actions. What happens though, **26)** _ _ _ _ those actions are wrong? Frank Serpico found a disturbing **27)** _ _ _ _ _ _ to that question. Serpico **28)** _ _ _ _ _ _ the New York City Police Department assuming **29)** _ _ _ _ high moral standards were typical of his fellow officers. When he **30)** _ _ _ _ _ out otherwise, he was faced with a dilemma: **31)** _ _ _ _ _ _ he violate the trust of his fellow officers by exposing the corruption, **32)** _ _ should he close his **33)** _ _ _ _ because loyalty to his **34)** _ _ _ _ _ _ officers outweighed all other moral (and legal) considerations? Serpico made his **35)** _ _ _ _ _ _. Public attention was focused on police **36)** _ _ _ _ _ _ _ _ _ _ and the NYPD was improved as a **37)** _ _ _ _ _ _, but those improvements came at a tremendous personal **38)** _ _ _ _ to Serpico. Ostracized and reviled by other officers, who felt **39)** _ _ _ _ _ _ _ _, Serpico eventually left the **40)** _ _ _ _ _.

ANSWER KEY
BOOK ONE

PART ONE: CLARITY

1. a. Each of the other choices includes a sentence fragment.

2. c. The verb should be *was*, not *were*, to agree with *the guard*. The verbs in the second half of the sentence should be in the past tense, like the first half of the sentence.

3. c. The correct preposition is *of*. *Think that* in answers **b** and **d** would require a complete clause with a verb, rather than the phrase that actually completes the sentence.

4. d. The modifier *with a growl* should be placed next to *the masked gunman*.

5. b. *Bravest* is the correct form of the adjective.

6. d. The correct pronoun case forms are used in this choice; answer **a** contains a redundant subject (*My partner Rosie and I, we...*); **b** and **c** contain incorrect pronoun case forms.

7. a. The modifier *a sharpshooter for many years* is clearly and correctly placed only in this choice.

8. b. The correct preposition is *by*; **a**, **c**, and **d** contain incorrect prepositions: *of*, *off of*, and *from*.

9. a. The subject *recession* agrees in number with its verb *is*; in the other choices, the subjects and verbs do not agree.

10. a. The other choices are unclear because they are awkwardly constructed, obscuring who intends to set the fire.

11. c. The other choices contain unnecessary shifts in person, from *people* to *their* and *we* in answer **a**, to *your* and *one* in answer **b**, and to *our* and *they* in answer **d**.

12. d. This is the only answer in which subject and verb agree.

13. a. The verb *is* agrees with its noun *neither*.

14. c. There is no unnecessary shift in tense between *are* in the first half of the sentence and *is* in the second half; in the other choices there are unnecessary shifts in tense.

15. b. *Herself* is the proper pronoun because it refers to something Sgt. Ahlamady does *for herself*, but there is no reason for the speaker to refer to *myself*. Incorrect pronouns are used in the other choices.

PART TWO: VOCABULARY

Consult a dictionary if you're not sure why the answers for vocabulary and spelling questions are correct.

16. c.
17. a.
18. d.
19. c.
20. d.
21. b.
22. d.
23. a.
24. a.
25. b.
26. d.
27. b.
28. a.
29. b.
30. a.

PART THREE: SPELLING

31. a.
32. b.
33. b.
34. d.
35. c.
36. d.
37. c.
38. b.
39. d.
40. a.
41. d.
42. a.
43. b.
44. d.
45. d.

PART FOUR: READING COMPREHENSION

46. a. The discussion of the traits of a person with anti-social personality disorder in the middle of the passage specifies that such a person does not have distortions of thought. The passage speaks of the anti-social person as being "inordinately self-confident" (b) and of the person's "emotional shallowness" (c and d).

47. d. The third sentence of the passage speaks of "con games." None of the other professions would suit an impulsive, shallow person who has been in trouble with the law.

48. b. The passage mentions "emotional shallowness." The other choices hint at the capability to feel meaningful emotion.

49. b. The passage says that a person with anti-social personality disorder can mimic real emotion, thereby conning prison officials, judges, and psychiatrists. The other choices are mentioned in the passage, but not in connection with getting out of trouble with the law.

50. d. Although the last sentence expands on the main point, the rest of the passage explains why hearsay evidence is only admissible when it doesn't matter whether or not the statement is true.

51. a. This statement may be true, but it isn't in the passage.

52. b. See the last sentence of the passage.

53. d. The passage deals not only with the sphere of law but more centrally with the sphere of values and civil conduct. Nowhere does the passage say that police officers should be idealistic (answer c).

54. d. Fairness and accuracy, respect for individuals, and the importance of maintaining community relations are all mentioned in the second paragraph. Maintaining morale on a multiracial force is also important, but it is not mentioned in the passage.

55. a. See the first sentence of the second paragraph. Answer d is close, but the passage suggests a police officer must be not only an authority but also an exemplar.

56. c. See the second sentence of the second paragraph.

57. b. *Moderation* is explicitly referred to near the end of the second paragraph. *Justice* and *politeness* are synonymous with *fairness* and *civil conduct* in the passage. *Courage* is never mentioned.

58. c. The other choices, though mentioned in the passage, are not the main idea.

59. d. While keeping one's temper is probably an aspect of the program, it is not explicitly mentioned in the passage.

60. a. See the second sentence of the passage.

61. c. This idea is explicitly stated in the fourth sentence.

62. a. The criteria for using information about a witness to cast doubt on his or her testimony is the subject of the whole passage.

63. d. An accusation of spousal abuse would be prejudicial but not relevant to the question of the witness's truthfulness.

64. b. This prospect is raised in the last sentence.

65. c. A petty thief is not a felon.

BOOK TWO

1. high
2. college
3. time
4. no
5. costs
6. free
7. expensive
8. get
9. provide
10. who
11. best
12. than
13. lawbreakers
14. education

15. more
16. reason
17. way
18. deny
19. prison
20. they
21. bring
22. lives
23. officers
24. of
25. extremes
26. when
27. answer
28. joined

29. that
30. found
31. should
32. or
33. eyes
34. fellow
35. choice
36. corruption
37. result
38. cost
39. betrayed
40. force

SCORING

To pass the California POST test, you need a *score* of 70. But that 70 doesn't necessarily mean 70 questions right. The number of correct answers you need for a score of 70 changes each time the test is given. A good estimate of a passing score is 70%, or 74 questions right.

Take your score from this first practice exam and apply it to the self-evaluation section of the State Police Exam Planner in Chapter 4. A table there suggests what kind of preparation you should undertake based on your score on this exam.

But your total score isn't the main point right now. Analyzing your performance on the exam is much more important. Take a subscore of each of the categories of questions. Did you do better on reading questions than on clarity questions, or vice versa? Then you should spend more of your preparation time on the area in which you scored lower and less time on the area in which you scored well. If you did less well than you expected on the whole test, your overall reading skills are probably one reason. Lots of challenging reading between now and the time of the exam can make a difference in your score.

On the other hand, if you scored pretty well, you can feel confident as you undertake your preparation. (No, having a good score does *not* mean you shouldn't prepare. It means you don't have to prepare *a lot.*) You probably just need to brush up on a few things and continue to familiarize yourself with what's likely to be on the exam.

The chapters that follow this test focus on the areas tested in the California POST exams. These chapters offer helpful hints and advice for doing well on the various kinds of questions. Depending on your score on the test you just took, you might choose to breeze quickly through those chapters or really knuckle down and study hard. Either way, those chapters will give you what you need to score your best.

C·H·A·P·T·E·R 7

READING COMPREHENSION

CHAPTER SUMMARY

Reading is a vital skill for any potential law enforcement officer, so most civil service tests include reading comprehension questions. The tips and exercises in this chapter will help you improve your reading comprehension so that you can increase your score in this area.

Most civil service tests attempt to measure how well applicants understand what they read. Understanding written materials is part of almost any job, including law enforcement. The tests are usually in a multiple-choice format and have questions based on brief passages, much like the standardized tests that are offered in schools. For that matter, almost all standardized test questions test your reading skill. After all, you can't answer the question if you can't read it! Similarly, you can't study your course material at the academy or learn new procedures once you're on the job if you can't read well. So reading comprehension is vital not only on the test but also for the rest of your career.

TYPES OF READING COMPREHENSION QUESTIONS

You have probably encountered reading comprehension questions before, where you are given a passage to read and then have to answer multiple-choice questions about it. The advantages of these questions for you, the test taker, are that you don't have to know anything about the topic in the passage and that the answers are usually right there—if you just know where to find them. This leads to one of the disadvantages: you have to search quickly for answers in an unfamiliar text. It's easy to fall for one of the wrong answer choices, which may be designed to mislead you.

The best way to do well on this passage/question format is to be very familiar with the kinds of questions that are typically asked on the test. Questions most frequently ask you to:

1. identify a specific **fact or detail** in the passage
2. note the **main idea** of the passage
3. define a **vocabulary** word from the passage
4. make an **inference** based on the passage

PRACTICE PASSAGE 1: USING THE FOUR QUESTION TYPES

The following is a sample test passage, followed by four questions. Read the passage, and then answer the questions, based on your reading of the text, by circling your choice. Then note under your answer the letter of the type of question you believe each to be based on the list above. Correct answers appear immediately after the questions.

In the last decade, community policing has been frequently touted as the best way to reform urban law enforcement. The idea of putting more officers on foot patrol in high crime areas, where relations with police have frequently been strained, was initiated in Houston in 1983 under the leadership of then-Commissioner Lee Brown. He believed that officers should be accessible to the community at the street level. If officers were assigned to the same area over a period of time, those officers would eventually build a network of trust with neighborhood residents. That trust would mean that merchants and residents in the community would let officers know about criminal activities in the area and would support police intervention. Since then, many large cities have experimented with Community-Oriented Policing (COP) with mixed results. Some have found that police and citizens are grateful for the opportunity to work together. Others have found that unrealistic expectations by citizens and resistance from officers have combined to hinder the effectiveness of COP. It seems possible, therefore, that a good idea may need improvement before it can truly be considered a reform.

1.   Community policing has been used in law enforcement since
     a. the late 1970s
     b. the early 1980s
     c. the Carter administration
     d. Lee Brown was New York City Police Commissioner

     Question type_____

2. The phrase "a network of trust" in this passage suggests that
  a. police officers can rely only on each other for support
  b. community members rely on the police to protect them
  c. police and community members rely on each other
  d. community members trust only each other

Question type_____

3. The best title for this passage would be
  a. Community Policing: The Solution to the Drug Problem
  b. Houston Sets the Pace in Community Policing
  c. Communities and Cops: Partners for Peace
  d. Community Policing: An Uncertain Future?

Question type_____

4. The word "touted" in the first sentence of the passage most nearly means
  a. praised
  b. denied
  c. exposed
  d. criticized

Question type_____

ANSWERS AND EXPLANATIONS FOR PRACTICE PASSAGE 1

Don't just look at the right answers and move on. The explanations are the most important part. Use these explanations to help you understand how to tackle each kind of question the next time you come across it.

1. b. Question type: 1, fact or detail. The passage says that community policing began "in the last decade." A decade is a period of ten years. In addition, the passage identifies 1983 as the first large-scale use of community policing in Houston. Don't be misled by trying to figure out when Carter was president. Also, if you happen to know that Lee Brown was New York City's police commissioner, don't let that information lead you away from the information contained in the passage alone. Brown was commissioner in Houston when he initiated community policing.

2. c. Question type: 4, inference. The "network of trust" referred to in this passage is between the community and the police, as you can see from the sentence where the phrase appears. The key phrase in the question is *in this passage*. You may think that police can rely only on each other, or one of the other answer choices may appear equally plausible to you. But your choice of answers must be limited to the one suggested *in this passage*. Another tip for questions like this: Beware of absolutes! Be suspicious of any answer containing words like *only, always,* or *never.*

3. d. Question type: 2, main idea. The title always expresses the main idea. In this passage, the main idea comes at the end. The sum of all the details in the passage suggests that community policing is not without its critics and that therefore its future is uncertain. Another key phrase is *mixed* *results,* which means that some communities haven't had full success with community policing.

4. a. Question type: 3, vocabulary. The word *touted* is linked in this passage with the phrase *the best way to reform.* Most people would think that a good way to reform something is praiseworthy. In addition, the next few sentences in the passage describe the benefits of community policing. Criticism or a negative response to the subject doesn't come until later in the passage.

DETAIL AND MAIN IDEA QUESTIONS

Main idea questions and fact or detail questions are both asking you for information that's right there in the passage. All you have to do is find it.

DETAIL OR FACT QUESTIONS

In detail or fact questions, you have to identify a specific item of information from the test. This is usually the simplest kind of question. You just have to be able to separate important information from less important information. However, the choices may often be very similar, so you must be careful not to get confused.

MAIN IDEA QUESTIONS

The main idea of a passage, like that of a paragraph or a book, is what it is *mostly* about. The main idea is the summary of all the details. Sometimes the main idea is stated, often in the first or last sentence. Sometimes it is implied in the overall text. The key word in the definition is *mostly.* There may be much information in the passage. The trick is to understand what all that information adds up to—the gist of what the author wants us to know. Often some of the wrong answers on main idea questions are specific facts or details from the passage.

PRACTICE PASSAGE 2: DETAIL AND MAIN IDEA QUESTIONS

Practice answering main idea and detail questions by working on the questions that follow this passage. Circle the answers to the questions, and then check your answers against the key that appears immediately after the questions.

There is some evidence that crime rates are linked to social trends such as demographic and socio-economic changes. Crime statistics showed a decline in the post-World War II era of the 1940s and 50s. Following the Vietnam War in the 1970s, however, reported crimes were on the rise again, only to be followed by lower numbers of such reports in the 1980s. One of the reasons for these fluctuations appears to be age. When the population is younger, as in the 1960s when the baby boomers came of age, there was a greater incidence of crime nationwide. A second cause for the rise and fall of crime rates appears to be economic. Rising crime rates appear to follow falling economies. A third cause cited for the cyclical nature of crime statistics appears to be the ebb and flow of public policy decisions, which sometimes protect personal freedoms at the expense of government control. A youthful, economically disadvantaged population that is not secured by social controls of family and community or by government authority is likely to see an upswing in reported crimes.

1. Crime statistics seem to rise when populations are
   a. younger
   b. older
   c. veteran
   d. richer

Question type_____

2. The main idea of the passage is that
   a. times of prosperity show lower crime statistics
   b. when the economy slows, crime statistics rise
   c. incidence of reported crime is related to several social and economic variables
   d. secure families are less likely to be involved in crime

Question type_____

3. The best title for this passage would be
   a. Wars and Crime Statistics
   b. Why Crime Statistics Rise and Fall
   c. Youth and Crime Statistics
   d. Poverty and Crime Statistics

Question type_____

4. Crime statistics show that crime is
   a. random
   b. cyclical
   c. demographic
   d. social

Question type_____

ANSWERS AND EXPLANATIONS FOR PRACTICE PASSAGE 2

1. a. Question type: 1, detail. This is a fairly clear example of how you can look quickly through a passage and locate a clearly stated detail. The word *young* appears in relation to the baby boomers; the idea is also suggested in the last sentence by the word *youthful*.

2. c. Question type: 2, main idea. The other answer choices are details—they're all in the passage, but they're not what the passage is *mostly* about. Answer **c** is the only one that combines several details into a statement that reflects the first sentence, which is also the topic sentence, of the paragraph.

3. b. Question type: 2, main idea. Each of the other choices expresses a detail, one of the reasons listed in the passage for fluctuation in crime rates. Answer **b** is the only one that expresses the sum of those details.

4. b. Question type: 1, detail. The passage mentions "the cyclical nature of crime statistics." Other phrases that suggest this answer include *fluctuations, rise and fall,* and *ebb and flow.*

VOCABULARY AND INFERENCE QUESTIONS

Questions that ask you about the meaning of vocabulary words in the passage and those that ask what the passage *suggests* or *implies* (inference questions) are different from detail or main idea questions. In vocabulary and inference questions, you usually have to pull ideas from the passage, sometimes from more than one place in the passage.

VOCABULARY QUESTIONS

Questions designed to test vocabulary are really trying to measure how well you can figure out the meaning of an unfamiliar word simply by making a good association based on context. Theoretically you should be able to substitute a nonsense word for the one being sought, and you would still make the right choice because you could determine meaning strictly from the sense of the sentence. Try to determine the meaning of this nonsense word from the rest of the sentence:

> The chief noted that it gave him great *terivinix* to announce the award for Officer of the Year.

In this sentence, *terivinix* most likely means

  a. pain
  b. sympathy
  c. pleasure
  d. anxiety

Clearly, the context of an award makes **c**, *pleasure*, the best choice. Awards don't usually bring pain, sympathy, or anxiety. When confronted with an unfamiliar word, try substituting a nonsense word and see if the context gives you the clue.

INFERENCE QUESTIONS

Inference questions can be the most difficult to answer because they require you to take meaning from the text even when that meaning is not directly stated. Inferences are hints that we take based on the clues the writer has given us. You have to read between the lines in order to make a judgment about what an author was implying in the passage.

PRACTICE PASSAGE 3: VOCABULARY AND INFERENCE QUESTIONS

The questions that follow this passage are strictly vocabulary and inference questions. Circle the answers to the questions, and then check your answers against the key that appears immediately after the questions.

In recent years, issues of public and personal safety have become a major concern to many Americans. Violent incidents in fast-food restaurants, libraries, hospitals, schools, and offices have led many to seek greater security inside and outside of their homes. Sales of burglar alarms and high-tech security devices such as motion detectors and video monitors have skyrocketed in the last decade. Convenience stores and post offices have joined banks and jewelry stores in barricading staff behind iron bars and safety glass enclosures. Communities employ private security forces and encourage homeowners to keep trained attack dogs on their premises. While some people have sympathy for the impetus behind these efforts, there is also some concern that these measures will create a "siege mentality" leading to general distrust among people that could foster a dangerous isolationism within neighborhoods and among neighbors.

1. The passage suggests which of the following about community security?
   a. Communities are more dangerous today than they were ten years ago.
   b. Too much concern for security can destroy trust among neighbors.
   c. Poor security has led to an increase in public violence.
   d. Isolated neighborhoods are safe neighborhoods.

Question type_____

2. The word "foster" in the last sentence of the passage most nearly means
   a. adopt
   b. encourage
   c. prevent
   d. secure

Question type_____

3. The author believes that
   a. more security is needed to make neighborhoods safer
   b. people should spend more on home security
   c. people should not ignore the problems created by excessive safety concerns
   d. attack dogs and high-tech devices are the best protection against violent crime

Question type_____

4. In the last sentence, the phrase "siege mentality" means
   a. hostility
   b. defensiveness
   c. fear
   d. corruption

Question type_____

ANSWERS AND EXPLANATIONS FOR PRACTICE PASSAGE 3

1. **b.** Question type; 4, inference. The key word here is *distrust,* which implies that neighbors become suspicious of each other if they are worried about safety.

2. **b.** Question type: 3, vocabulary. The first answer choice is meant to confuse you if you associate the word *foster* with foster care and, by extension, with adoption. *Foster* means *nurture* or *help to grow.* Look again at the sentence. What could *a general distrust*—the thing that fosters—do to *a dangerous isolationism*—the thing being fostered? A general distrust could *encourage* a dangerous isolationism.

3. **c.** Question type: 4, inference. By using phrases like *dangerous isolationism,* the author suggests that he or she doesn't approve of the move toward more use of security devices. The other answer choices all indicate the author's approval of the trend being discussed.

4. **b.** Question type: 3, vocabulary. The key word here is *siege.* People who perceive themselves to be under attack tend to stick together in the face of a common enemy. They become quick to defend themselves against that enemy.

If English Isn't Your First Language

One of the difficulties of taking reading tests for non-native English speakers is the lack of a frame of reference that allows for quick comprehension of the text. People who have not lived in or been educated in the U.S. often don't have the background information that comes from reading American newspapers, magazines, and textbooks.

A second problem for non-native English speakers is the difficulty in recognizing vocabulary and idioms that assist comprehension. In order to read with good understanding, the test taker must have an immediate grasp of as many words as possible in the text.

The Long View

Read newspapers, magazines, and other periodicals that deal with current events and matters of local, state, and national importance. Pay special attention to articles related to law enforcement issues.

Be alert to new or unfamiliar vocabulary or terms that occur frequently in the popular press. Get a highlighter pen and use it to pick out new or unfamiliar words as you read. Keep a list of those words and their definitions. Review them for 15 minutes each day.

During the Test

When you are taking the test, make a picture in your mind of the situation being described in the passage. Ask yourself, "What did the writer mostly want me to think about this subject?"

Locate and underline the topic sentence which carries the main idea of the passage. Remember that the topic sentence may not always be the first sentence.

REVIEW: PUTTING IT ALL TOGETHER

A good way to solidify what you've learned about reading comprehension questions is for *you* to write the questions. Here's a passage, followed by space for you to write your own questions. Write one question of each of the four types: fact or detail, main idea, vocabulary, and inference.

In recent years law enforcement officers have welcomed the advent of a number of new technologies which have aided them greatly in their work. These include long-range eavesdropping devices and computer scanners that allow police to identify possible suspects by merely typing a license number into a computer in the patrol car. The scanner allows instant access to motor vehicle and criminal records and gives officers the opportunity to snare wrongdoers, even when they are not involved in criminal activity at the time. Police departments have praised the use of the computers, which they say help them get criminals off the streets and out of the way of honest citizens. Not all of those citizens agree with this attitude, however; some believe that arrests made solely on the basis of scanner identification constitute an invasion of privacy. They regard the accessing of records as illegal search and seizure. In New Jersey, Florida, and Arizona, lawsuits have been filed by citizens who believe that their constitutional rights have been violated. They believe that much computer-generated information is inaccurate and vulnerable to computer hackers who invade computer data bases. Some believe that such information from scanners could be used to charge innocent citizens with crimes or to target particular neighborhoods for harassment.

1. Detail question:_____
   a.
   b.
   c.
   d.

2. Main idea question:_____
   a.
   b.
   c.
   d.

3. Inference question_____
   a.
   b.
   c.
   d.

4. Vocabulary question_____
   a.
   b.
   c.
   d.

Possible Questions

Here is one question of each type based on the passage above. Your questions may be very different, but these will give you an idea of the kinds of questions that could be asked.

1. Main idea question: Which of the following best expresses the main idea of the passage?
   a. New technologies are available to police officers.
   b. Police are skeptical of new policing technologies.
   c. New technologies raise questions of privacy.
   d. New technologies may be discriminatory.

2. Detail question: Computer scanners allow police to
   a. identify suspects
   b. access computer databases
   c. locate wrongdoers
   d. all of the above

3. Vocabulary question: In this passage the word "snare" means
   a. question
   b. interrupt
   c. capture
   d. free

4. Inference question: The writer implies, but does not directly state, that
   a. computer technologies must be used with care
   b. high-tech policing is the wave of the future
   c. most citizens believe that high-tech policing is beneficial
   d. most police officers prefer using the new technologies

HOW TO ANSWER FILL-IN-THE-BLANK READING QUESTIONS

Some exams test your reading skills by having you fill in the missing words in a reading passage. To do well, you need both good reading skills and good test-taking skills. Below are some tips to help you sharpen your test-taking techniques.

FINDING THE MISSING WORD

You will be given reading passages with words omitted. Each missing word is indicated by a series of dashes. There is one dash for each letter in the missing word. You will have to determine the missing words and mark them correctly on your answer sheet. Here's how:

- Read the paragraph through quickly to get the general idea of it.
- Now go back to fill in the blanks by putting one letter on each line. Do the easy words first, then work on the harder ones. Choose only one word for each blank space. Make sure that word has exactly as many letters as there are dashes *and* makes sense in the sentence.
- Try to fill in every blank. Guess if you have to.
- Don't be alarmed if you're not sure of some of your answers. You can miss several words and still do well.

Look at the following sample sentence:

Fortunately, no one was hurt when the _ _ _ _ _ was derailed.

There are five dashes so the word you need must have five letters. The correct answer is **train** because it makes sense and has five letters. The word *engine* makes sense in the sentence, but it is incorrect because it is not a five-letter word. *Plane* is a five-letter word but is incorrect because planes cannot be derailed. Write the word *train* in the blank space.

MARKING THE ANSWER SHEET

Once you have completed the passage, you will have to mark your answers on the answer sheet. On the answer sheet, you will find numbered columns. Each column contains the letters A–Z, and the number at the top of the column corresponds to the number of a missing word in the passage. To mark your answer on the answer sheet, print the **first letter** of the word you wrote in the blank space in the passage in the box directly under the appropriate item number. Then, completely blacken the circle in that column containing the letter you wrote in the box.

....

IMPORTANT:

The words you wrote in the blank spaces in the passage will not be scored. Neither will the letters you write at the top of the columns on the answer sheet. Only the darkened circles of the letters you have chosen will be scored. Make sure you mark your answers correctly.

....

As you mark your answer sheet, check to make sure that:

1. the item number on the answer sheet is the same as the item number in the passage
2. you have written the correct first letter in the box
3. you have completely blackened the correct circle below the box

For example, if you chose *train* as the first missing word in a passage, you would find column 1, print T in the box, and blacken the circle with T in it.

PRACTICE FILL-IN-THE-BLANK PASSAGE

Now read the following sample paragraph.

Fortunately, no one was hurt when the 1)_ _ _ _ _
was derailed. The derailment occurred 2)_ _ _ _ _ _ _
lumber and other debris were piled on the tracks.
Investigators believe a 3)_ _ _ _ _ _ of people were
involved. They are looking into the possibility
4)_ _ _ _ a local gang caused the accident for 5)_ _ _.
It would not be the first 6)_ _ _ _ that members of
this 7)_ _ _ _ caused serious damage.

First write the answers in the blank spaces (one letter
per line), then mark them on the answer sheet below.
Work as quickly as you can without sacrificing accuracy. Double check often to be sure you are marking
your answers correctly. See the end of the chapter for
answers.

	1	2	3	4	5	6	7	8	9	10
WRITE 1ST LETTER OF WORD HERE										

WRITE 1ST LETTER OF WORD HERE

A A A A A A A A A A
B B B B B B B B B B
C C C C C C C C C C
D D D D D D D D D D
E E E E E E E E E E
F F F F F F F F F F
G G G G G G G G G G
H H H H H H H H H H
I I I I I I I I I I
J J J J J J J J J J
K K K K K K K K K K
L L L L L L L L L L

CODE LETTERS HERE

M M M M M M M M M M
N N N N N N N N N N
O O O O O O O O O O
P P P P P P P P P P
Q Q Q Q Q Q Q Q Q Q
R R R R R R R R R R
S S S S S S S S S S
T T T T T T T T T T
U U U U U U U U U U
V V V V V V V V V V
W W W W W W W W W W
X X X X X X X X X X
Y Y Y Y Y Y Y Y Y Y
Z Z Z Z Z Z Z Z Z Z

ADDITIONAL RESOURCES

Here are some other ways you can build the vocabulary and knowledge that will help you do well on reading comprehension questions.

- Practice asking the four sample question types about passages you read for information or pleasure.
- If you belong to a computer network such as America Online or Compuserve, search out articles related to law enforcement. Exchange views with others on the Internet. All of these exchanges will contribute to the knowledge needed to relate to the passage material on the tests.
- Use your library. Many public libraries have sections, sometimes called "Lifelong Learning Centers," that contain materials for adult learners. In these sections you can find books with exercises in reading and study skills. It's also a good idea to enlarge your base of information about the criminal justice field by reading books and articles on subjects related to criminology. Many libraries have computer systems that allow you to access information quickly and easily. Library personnel will show you how to use the computers and microfilm and microfiche machines.
- Begin now to build a broad knowledge of the law enforcement profession. Get in the habit of reading articles in newspapers and magazines on law enforcement issues. Keep a clipping file of those articles. This will help keep you informed of trends in the profession and aware of pertinent vocabulary related to policing issues.
- Consider reading or subscribing to professional journals. The journals listed below are written for

a general readership among law-enforcement personnel and are available for a reasonable annual fee. They may also be available in your public library.

Corrections Today
American Correctional Association
4380 Forbes Boulevard
Lanham, MD 20706

FBI Law Enforcement Bulletin
Madison Building, Rm. 209
FBI Academy
Quantico, VA 22135

Law and Order
Hendon, Inc.
1000 Skokie Boulevard
Willamette, IL 60091

Police Chief
International Association of Chiefs of Police, Inc.
515 North Washington Street
Alexandria, VA 22314

Police: The Law Officer's Magazine
Hare Publications
P.O. Box 847
Carlsbad, CA 92018

If you need more help building your reading skills and taking reading comprehension tests, consider *Improve Your Reading Comprehension in 20 Minutes a Day* by Judith Meyers, published by LearningExpress. Order information is in the back of this book.

ANSWERS TO FILL-IN-THE-BLANK READING QUESTIONS

1. train
2. because
3. number
4. that
5. fun
6. time
7. gang

C · H · A · P · T · E · R

GRAMMAR

8

CHAPTER SUMMARY

This chapter reviews the sentence-level writing skills often tested on multiple-choice exams, including complete sentences, capitalization, punctuation, subject-verb agreement, verb tenses, pronouns, and confusing word pairs.

An effective law enforcement professional needs to know how to use a variety of tools well to do a good job. Probably few of the tools are as important or will be used as often as written language. Knowing how to use written language is vital, not just for the exam, but for your career. This chapter covers the smaller, sentence-level grammatical and mechanical aspects of writing well.

COMPLETE SENTENCES

Sentences are the basic unit of written language. Most writing is done using complete sentences, so it's important to distinguish sentences from fragments. A sentence expresses a complete thought, while a fragment requires something more to express a complete thought.

Look at the following pairs of word groups. The first in each pair is a sentence fragment; the second is a complete sentence.

COMPLETE SENTENCES

Fragment	Complete Sentence
The dog walking down the street.	The dog was walking down the street.
Exploding from the bat for a home run.	The ball exploded from the bat for a home run.

These examples show that a sentence must have a subject and a verb to complete its meaning. The first fragment has a subject, but not a verb. *Walking* looks like a verb, but it is actually an adjective describing *dog*. The second fragment has neither a subject nor a verb. *Exploding* looks like a verb, but it too is an adjective describing something not identified in the word group.

Now look at the next set of word groups. Mark those that are complete sentences.

1.
   a. We saw the tornado approaching.
   b. When we saw the tornado approaching.

2.
   a. Before the house was built in 1972.
   b. The house was built in 1972.

3.
   a. Since we are leaving in the morning.
   b. We are leaving in the morning.

If you chose **1.a.**, **2.b.**, and **3.b.**, you were correct. You may have noticed that the groups of words are the same, but the fragments have an extra word at the beginning. These words are called subordinating conjunctions. If a group of words that would normally be a complete sentence is preceded by a subordinating conjunction, something more is needed to complete the thought.

- When we saw the tornado approaching, we headed for cover.
- Before the house was built in 1972, the old house was demolished.
- Since we were leaving in the morning, we went to bed early.

Here is a list of words that can be used as subordinating conjunctions.

after	that
although	though
as	unless
because	until
before	when
if	whenever
once	where
since	wherever
than	while

If you can tell when a group of words isn't a sentence, then you can tell when one or more sentences have been run together, sometimes with a comma in between. Some tests will ask you to find run-on sentences. Each of the sentences below is a run-on sentence. Can you find where to put a period and begin a new sentence?

1. We went to the beach, we had a good time.
2. Without exception, the prisoners conformed to the new ruling they kept their cells clean.
3. The defense needed time to examine the new evidence, the lawyer asked for an extension.

If you noticed that a new sentence begins after *beach* in the first sentence, after *ruling* in the second, and after *evidence* in the third, you were right. Generally, you can tell whether you're looking at a run-on by covering the second half of the sentence and asking yourself whether the first half by itself is a sentence. Then cover the first half. Is the second half a sentence by itself? If your answer to the first and/or second question is *no*, then the sentence is fine. If you answered both questions *yes*—both halves of the sentence could be sentences by themselves—then you've got a run-on, unless there happens to be a semicolon (;) between the two halves.

Some of the questions on a civil service exam may test your ability to distinguish a sentence from a fragment or a run-on. Check for a subject and a verb, as well as for subordinating conjunctions. Check yourself with the following sample questions. The answers are at the end of this chapter.

1. Which of the following groups of words is a complete sentence?
   a. The treasure buried beneath the floorboards beside the furnace.
   b. After we spent considerable time examining all of the possibilities before making a decision.
   c. In addition to the methods the doctor used to diagnose the problem.
   d. The historical account of the incident bore the most resemblance to fact.

2. Which of the following groups of words is a complete sentence?
   a. This was fun to do.
   b. We looking.
   c. Before the door opened.
   d. If we ever see you again.

3. Which of the following groups of words is a run-on?
   a. Whenever I see the moon rise, I am awed by the deep orange color.

   b. The special services unit completed its work and made its report to the chief.
   c. Unless we hear from the directors of the board before the next meeting, we will not act on the new proposal.
   d. We slept soundly we never heard the alarm.

CAPITALIZATION

You may encounter questions that test your ability to capitalize correctly. Here is a quick review of the most common capitalization rules.

- Capitalize the first word of a sentence. If the first word is a number, write it as a word.
- Capitalize the pronoun *I*.
- Capitalize the first word of a quotation: I said, "What's the name of your dog?" Do not capitalize the first word of a partial quotation: He called me "the worst excuse for a student" he had ever seen.
- Capitalize proper nouns and proper adjectives.

See the table on the next page.

The following passage contains no capitalized words. Circle those letters that should be capitalized.

when I first saw the black hills on january 2, 1995, i was shocked by their beauty. we had just spent new year's day in sioux falls, south dakota and had headed west toward our home in denver, colorado. as we traveled along interstate 90, i could see the black hills rising slightly in the distance. president calvin coolidge had called them "a wondrous sight to behold." i understood why. after driving through the badlands and stopping at wall drug in wall, south

CAPITALIZATION

Category	Example (Proper nouns)
days of the week, months of the year	Friday, Saturday; January, February
holidays, special events	Christmas, Halloween; Two Rivers Festival, Dilly Days
names of individuals	John Henry, George Billeck
names of structures, buildings	Lincoln Memorial, Principal Building
names of trains, ships, aircraft	Queen Elizabeth, Chicago El
product names	Corn King hams, Dodge Intrepid
cities and states	Des Moines, Iowa; Juneau, Alaska
streets, highways, roads	Grand Avenue, Interstate 29, Deadwood Road
landmarks, public areas	Continental Divide, Grand Canyon, Glacier National Park
bodies of water	Atlantic Ocean, Mississippi River
ethnic groups, languages, nationalities	Asian-American, English, Arab
official titles	Mayor Daley, President Johnson
institutions, organizations, businesses	Dartmouth College, Lions Club, Chrysler Corporation
proper adjectives	English muffin, Polish sausage

dakota, we liked the way the evergreen-covered hills broke the barren monotony of the landscape. my oldest daughter said, "dad, look! there's something that's not all white." we could see why the lakota sioux regarded them as a native american holy ground. we saw mount rushmore and custer state park, the home of the largest herd of buffalo in north america. we also drove the treacherous spearfish canyon road. fortunately, our jeep cherokee had no trouble with the ice and snow on the winding road.

Check your circled version against the corrected version of the passage below.

When I first saw the Black Hills on January 2, 1995, I was shocked by their beauty. We had just spent New Year's Day in Sioux Falls, South Dakota and had headed west toward our home in Denver, Colorado. As we traveled along Interstate 90, I could see the Black Hills rising slightly in the distance. President Calvin Coolidge had called them "a wondrous sight to behold." I understood why. After driving through the Badlands and stopping at Wall Drug in Wall, South Dakota, we liked the way the evergreen-covered hills broke the barren monotony of the landscape. My oldest daughter said, "Dad, look! There's something that's not all white." We could see why the Lakota Sioux regarded them as a Native American holy ground. We saw Mount Rushmore and Custer State Park, the home of the largest herd of buffalo in North America. We also drove the treacherous Spearfish Canyon Road. Fortunately, our Jeep Cherokee had no trouble with the ice and snow on the winding road.

Now try these sample questions. Choose the option that is capitalized correctly. Answers are at the end of the chapter.

4.
  a. This year we will celebrate christmas on Tuesday, December 25 in Manchester, Ohio.
  b. This year we will celebrate Christmas on Tuesday, December 25 in manchester, Ohio.
  c. This year we will celebrate Christmas on Tuesday, December 25 in Manchester, Ohio.
  d. This year we will celebrate christmas on Tuesday, December 25 in manchester, Ohio.

5.
  a. Abraham Adams made an appointment with Mayor Burns to discuss the building plans.
  b. Abraham Adams made an appointment with Mayor Burns to discuss the Building Plans.
  c. Abraham Adams made an appointment with mayor Burns to discuss the building plans.
  d. Abraham Adams made an appointment with mayor Burns to discuss the Building Plans.

6.
  a. Ms. Abigal Dornburg, M.D., was named head of the review board for Physicians Mutual.
  b. Ms. Abigal Dornburg, M.D., was named Head of the Review Board for Physicians Mutual.
  c. Ms. Abigal Dornburg, m.d. Was named head of the review board for Physicians mutual.
  d. Ms. Abigal dornburg, M.D., was named head of the review board for Physicians Mutual.

PUNCTUATION

PERIODS

Here is a quick review of the rules regarding the use of a period.

- Use a period at the end of a sentence that is not a question or an exclamation.
- Use a period after an initial in a name: Millard K. Furham
- Use a period after an abbreviation, unless the abbreviation is an acronym.
  Abbreviations: Mr., Ms., Dr., A.M., General Motors Corp., Allied Inc.
  Acronyms: NASA, AIDS
- If a sentence ends with an abbreviation, use only one period. (We brought food, tents, sleeping bags, etc.)

COMMAS

Using commas correctly can make the difference between presenting information clearly and distorting the facts. The following chart demonstrates the necessity of commas in written language. How many people are listed in the sentence?

COMMAS AND MEANING	
Number undetermined	My sister Diane John Carey Melissa and I went to the fair.
Four people	My sister Diane, John Carey, Melissa, and I went to the fair.
Five people	My sister, Diane, John Carey, Melissa, and I went to the fair.
Six people	My sister, Diane, John, Carey, Melissa, and I went to the fair.

Here is a quick review of the most basic rules regarding the use of commas.

- Use a comma before *and, but, or, for, nor,* and *yet* when they separate two groups of words that could be complete sentences.
  Example: The coaches laid out the game plan, and the team executed it to perfection.
- Use a comma to separate items in a series.
  Example: The student driver stopped, looked, and listened when she got to the railroad tracks.
- Use a comma to separate two or more adjectives modifying the same noun.
  Example: The hot, black, rich coffee tasted great after an hour in below-zero weather. [Notice that there is no comma between *rich* (an adjective) and *coffee* (the noun *rich* describes)].
- Use a comma after introductory words, phrases, or clauses in a sentence.

Examples: Usually, the class begins with a short writing assignment. [Word]
Racing down the street, the yellow car ran a stoplight. [Phrase]
After we found the source of the noise, we relaxed and enjoyed the rest of the evening. [Clause]
- Use a comma after a name followed by Jr., Sr., or some other abbreviation.
  Example: The class was inspired by the speeches of Martin Luther King, Jr.
- Use a comma to separate items in an address.
  Example: The car stopped at 1433 West G Avenue, Orlando, Florida 36890.
- Use a comma to separate a day and a year, as well as after the year.
  Example: I was born on July 21, 1954, during a thunderstorm.
- Use a comma after the greeting of a friendly letter and after the closing of any letter.
  Example: Dear Uncle Jon,
  Sincerely yours,
- Use a comma to separate contrasting elements in a sentence.
  Example: Your essay needs strong arguments, not strong opinions, to convince me.
- Use commas to set off appositives (words or phrases that explain or identify a noun).
  Example: My cat, a Siamese, is named Ron.

The following passage contains no commas or periods. Add commas and periods as needed.

Dr Newton Brown Jr a renowned chemist has held research positions for OPEC Phillips Petroleum Inc Edward L Smith Chemical Designs and R J Reynolds Co His thorough exhaustive research is recognized in academic circles as well as in the business community as the most well-designed reliable data available Unfortunately on July 6 1988 he retired after a brief but serious illness He lives in a secluded retirement community at 2401 Beach Sarasota Springs Florida

Check your version against the corrected version below.

Dr. Newton Brown, Jr., a renowned chemist, has held research positions for OPEC, Phillips Petroleum Inc., Edward L. Smith Chemical Designs, and R. J. Reynolds Co. His thorough, exhaustive research is recognized in academic circles, as well as in the business community, as the most well-designed, reliable data available. Unfortunately, on July 6, 1988, he retired after a brief, but serious illness. He lives in a secluded retirement community at 2401 Beach, Sarasota Springs, Florida.

APOSTROPHES

Apostrophes communicate important information in written language. Here is a quick review of the two most important rules regarding the use of apostrophes.

- Use an apostrophe to show that letters have been omitted from a word to form a contraction.

Examples: do not = don't; national = nat'l; I will = I'll; it is = it's

- Use an apostrophe to show possession.

Check yourself with these sample test questions. Choose which of the four options is punctuated correctly. Answers are at the end of the chapter.

7.

a. Although it may seem strange, my partners purpose in interviewing Dr. E. S. Sanders Jr. was to eliminate him as a suspect in the crime.

b. Although it may seem strange my partner's purpose in interviewing Dr. E. S. Sanders, Jr. was to eliminate him, as a suspect in the crime.

c. Although it may seem strange, my partner's purpose in interviewing Dr. E. S. Sanders, Jr., was to eliminate him as a suspect in the crime.

d. Although it may seem strange, my partner's purpose in interviewing Dr. E. S. Sanders, Jr. was to eliminate him, as a suspect in the crime.

APOSTROPHES TO SHOW POSSESSION		
Singular nouns (add 's)	**Plural nouns ending in s (add ')**	**Plural nouns not ending in s**
boy's	boys'	men's
child's	kids'	children's
lady's	ladies'	women's

8.

   a. After colliding with a vehicle at the intersection of Grand, and Forest Ms. Anderson saw a dark hooded figure crawl through the window, reach back and grab a small parcel, and run north on Forest.

   b. After colliding with a vehicle at the intersection of Grand, and Forest, Ms. Anderson saw a dark hooded figure crawl through the window, reach back and grab a small parcel, and run north on Forest.

   c. After colliding with a vehicle at the intersection of Grand and Forest Ms. Anderson saw a dark, hooded figure crawl through the window, reach back and grab a small parcel, and run north on Forest.

   d. After colliding with a vehicle at the intersection of Grand and Forest, Ms. Anderson saw a dark, hooded figure crawl through the window, reach back and grab a small parcel, and run north on Forest.

9.

   a. When we interviewed each of the boys and the fathers, we determined that the men's stories did not match the boy's versions.

   b. When we interviewed each of the boys and the fathers, we determined that the men's stories did not match the boys' versions.

   c. When we interviewed each of the boys and the fathers, we determined that the mens' stories did not match the boys' versions.

   d. When we interviewed each of the boys' and the fathers', we determined that the men's stories did not match the boys' versions.

VERBS

SUBJECT-VERB AGREEMENT

In written language a subject must agree with its verb in number. In other words, if a subject is singular, the verb must be singular. If the subject is plural, the verb must be plural. If you are unsure whether a verb is singular or plural, apply this simple test. Fill in the blanks in the two sentences below with the matching form of the verb. The verb form that best completes the first sentence is singular. The verb form that best completes the second sentence is plural.

One person _____. [Singular]
Two people _____. [Plural]

Look at these examples using the verbs *speak* and *do*. Try it yourself with any verb that confuses you.

One person *speaks.*   One person *does.*
Two people *speak.*   Two people *do.*

Pronoun Subjects

Few people have trouble matching noun subjects and verbs, but pronouns are sometimes difficult for even the most sophisticated speakers of English. Some pronouns are always singular, others are always plural, still others can be both singular and plural.

These pronouns are always singular.

each	everyone
either	no one
neither	nobody
anybody	one
anyone	somebody
everybody	someone

The indefinite pronouns *each, either,* and *neither* are the ones most often misused. You can avoid a mismatch by mentally adding the word *one* after the pronoun and removing the other words between the pronoun and the verb. Look at the following examples.

Each **of the men** wants his own car.
Each **one** wants his own car.

Either **of the salesclerks** knows where the sale merchandise is located.
Either **one** knows where the sale merchandise is located.

These sentences may sound awkward because many speakers misuse these pronouns, and you are probably used to hearing them used incorrectly. Despite that, the substitution trick (*one* for the words following the pronoun) will help you avoid this mistake.

Some pronouns are always plural and require a plural verb:

both	many
few	several

Other pronouns can be either singular or plural:

all	none
any	some
most	

The words or prepositional phrases following them determine whether they are singular or plural. If what follows the pronouns is plural, the verb must be plural. If what follows is singular, the verb must be singular.

All of the **work is** finished.
All of the **jobs are** finished.

Is **any** of the **pizza** left?
Are **any** of the **pieces** of pizza left?

None of the **time was** wasted.
None of the **minutes were** wasted.

Subjects Joined by *and*

If two nouns or pronouns are joined by *and*, they require a plural verb.

He and she want to buy a new house.
Jack and Jill want to buy a new house.

Subjects Joined by *or* or *nor*

If two nouns or pronouns are joined by *or* or *nor*, they require a singular verb. Think of them as two separate sentences and you'll never make a mistake in agreement.

He or she wants to buy a new house.
　He wants to buy a new house.
　She wants to buy a new house.

Neither Jack nor Jill wants to buy a new house.
　Jack wants not to buy a new house.
　Jill wants not to buy a new house.

Circle the correct verb in each of the following sentences. Answers are at the end of the chapter.

10. Every other day either Bert or Ernie (takes, take) out the trash.

11. A woman in one of my classes (works, work) at the Civic Center box office.

12. A good knowledge of the rules (helps, help) you understand the game.

13. Each of these prescriptions (causes, cause) bloating and irritability.

14. (Have, Has) either of them ever arrived on time?

VERB TENSE

The tense of a verb tells a reader when the action occurs. Present tense verbs tell the reader to imagine that action happening as it is being read, while past tense verbs tell the reader the action has already happened. Read the following two paragraphs. The first one is written in the present tense, the second in the past tense. Notice the difference in the verbs. They are highlighted to make them easier to locate.

As Horace **opens** the door, he **glances** around cautiously. He **sees** signs of danger everywhere. The centerpiece and placemats from the dining room table **are scattered** on the floor next to the table. An end table in the living room **is lying** on its side. He **sees** the curtains flapping and **notices** glass on the carpet in front of the window.

As Horace **opened** the door, he **glanced** around cautiously. He **saw** signs of danger everywhere. The centerpiece and placemats from the dining room table **were scattered** on the floor next to the table. An end table in the living room **was lying** on its side. He **saw** the curtains flapping and **noticed** glass on the carpet in front of the window.

It's easy to distinguish present tense from past tense by simply fitting the verb into a sentence.

VERB TENSE

Present tense (Today, I ___ . . .)	Past tense (Yesterday, I ___ . . .)
drive	drove
think	thought
rise	rose
catch	caught

The important thing to remember about verb tense is to keep it consistent. If a passage begins in the present tense, keep it in the present tense unless there is a specific reason to change—to indicate that some action occurred in the past, for instance. If a passage begins in the past tense, it should remain in the past tense. Verb tense should never be mixed as it is in the following sentence.

Wrong: Terry **opens** the door and **saw** the crowd.
Correct: Terry **opens** the door and **sees** the crowd. Terry **opened** the door and **saw** the crowd.

However, sometimes it is necessary to use a different verb tense in order to clarify when an action occurred. Read the following sentences and the explanations following them.

The game warden **sees** the fish that you **caught**. [The verb **sees** is in the present tense, indicating that the action is occurring in the present. However, the verb **caught** is in the past tense, indicating that the fish were caught at some earlier time.]

The house that **was built** over a century ago **sits** on top of the hill. [The verb phrase **was built** is in the past tense, indicating that the house was built in the past. However, the verb **sits** is in the present tense, indicating that the action is still occurring.]

Check yourself with these sample questions. Choose the option that uses verb tense correctly. Answers are at the end of the chapter.

15.
   a. When I cry, I always get what I want.
   b. When I cry, I always got what I want.
   c. When I cried, I always got what I want.
   d. When I cried, I always get what I wanted.

16.
   a. It all started after I came home and am in my room studying for a big test.
   b. It all started after I came home and was in my room studying for a big test.
   c. It all starts after I come home and was in my room studying for a big test.
   d. It all starts after I came home and am in my room studying for a big test.

17.
   a. The child became excited and dashes into the house and slams the door.
   b. The child becomes excited and dashed into the house and slammed the door.
   c. The child becomes excited and dashes into the house and slammed the door.
   d. The child became excited and dashed into the house and slammed the door.

PRONOUNS

PRONOUN CASE

Most of the time, a single pronoun in a sentence is easy to use correctly. In fact, most English speakers would readily identify the mistakes in the following sentences.

Me went to the movie with **he**.
My teacher gave **she** a ride to school.

Most people know that **Me** in the first sentence should be **I** and that **he** should be **him**. They would also know that **she** in the second sentence should be **her**. Such errors are easy to spot when the pronouns are used alone in a sentence. The problem occurs when a pronoun is used with a noun or another pronoun. See if you can spot the errors in the following sentences.

The director rode with Jerry and I.
Belle and **him** are going to the ice arena.

The errors in these sentences are not as easy to spot as those in the sentences with a single pronoun. The easiest way to attack this problem is to turn the sentence with two pronouns into two separate sentences. Then the error once again becomes very obvious.

The director rode with Jerry.
The director rode with **me** (not I).

Belle is going to the ice arena. [Notice the singular verb *is* in place of *are*.]
He (not him) is going to the ice arena.

PRONOUN AGREEMENT

Another common error in using pronouns involves singular and plural pronouns. Like subjects and verbs, pronouns must match the number of the nouns they represent. If the noun a pronoun represents is singular, the pronoun must be singular. On the other hand, if the noun a pronoun represents is plural, the pronoun must be plural. Sometimes a pronoun represents another pronoun. If so, either both pronouns must be singular or both pronouns must be plural. Consult the list of singular and plural pronouns you saw earlier in this chapter.

The **doctor** must take a break when **she** (or **he**) is tired. [singular]
Doctors must take breaks when **they** are tired. [plural]

One of the girls misplaced **her** purse. [singular]
All of the girls misplaced **their** purses. [Plural]

If two or more singular nouns or pronouns are joined by *and,* use a plural pronoun to represent them.

Buddha and Muhammad built religions around **their** philosophies.
If **he and she** want to know where I was, **they** should ask me.

If two or more singular nouns or pronouns are joined by *or,* use a singular pronoun. If a singular and a plural noun or pronoun are joined by *or,* the pronoun agrees with the closest noun or pronoun it represents.

Matthew or Jacob will loan you **his** calculator.
The elephant or the moose will furiously protect **its** young.

Neither **the soldiers** nor **the sergeant** was sure of **his** location.
Neither **the sergeant** nor **the soldiers** were sure of **their** location.

Circle the correct pronoun in the following sentences. Answers are at the end of the chapter.

18. Andy or Arvin will bring (his, their) camera so (he, they) can take pictures of the party.

19. One of the file folders isn't in (its, their) drawer.

20. The NAPA store sent Bob and Ray the parts (he, they) had ordered.

21. Benny and (he, him) went to the movies with Bonnie and (I, me).

22. Neither my cousins nor my uncle knows what (he, they) will do tomorrow.

EASILY CONFUSED WORD PAIRS

The following words pairs are often misused in written language. By reading the explanations and looking at the examples, you can learn to use them correctly every time.

Its/it's

Its is a possessive pronoun that means "belonging to it." *It's* is a contraction for *it is* or *it has.* The only time you will ever use *it's* is when you can also substitute the words *it is* or *it has.*

Who/that

Who refers to people. *That* refers to things.

There is the man **who** helped me find a new pet.
The woman **who** invented the copper-bottomed kettle died in 1995.

This is the house **that** Harold bought.

The magazine **that** I needed was no longer in print.

There/their/they're

Their is a possessive pronoun that shows ownership. *There* is an adverb that tells where an action or item is located. *They're* is a contraction for the words *they are*. Here is an easy way to remember these words.

- *Their* means "belonging to them." Of the three words, *their* can be most easily transformed into the word *them*. Extend the *r* on the right side and connect the *i* and the *r* to turn *their* into *them*. This clue will help you remember that *their* means "belonging to them."
- If you examine the word *there*, you can see from the way it's written that it contains the word *here*. Whenever you use *there*, you should be able to substitute *here*. The sentence should still make sense.
- Imagine that the apostrophe in *they're* is actually a very small letter *a*. Use *they're* in a sentence only when you can substitute *they are*.

Your/you're

Your is a possessive pronoun that means "belonging to you." *You're* is a contraction for the words *you are*. The only time you will ever use *you're* is when you can also substitute the words *you are*.

To/too/two

To is a preposition or an infinitive.

- As a preposition: to the mall, to the bottom, to my church, to our garage, to his school, to his hideout, to our disadvantage, to an open room, to a ballad, to the gymnasium

- As an infinitive (*to* followed by a verb, sometimes separated by adverbs): to walk, to leap, to see badly, to find, to advance, to read, to build, to sorely want, to badly misinterpret, to carefully peruse

Too means "also." Whenever you use the word *too*, substitute the word *also*. The sentence should still make sense.

Two is a number, as in one, two. If you give it any thought at all, you'll never misuse this form.

The key is to think consciously about these words when you see them in written language. Circle the correct form of these easily confused words in the following sentences. Answers are at the end of the chapter.

23. (Its, It's) (to, too, two) late (to, too,two) remedy the problem now.

24. This is the man (who, that) helped me find the book I needed.

25. (There, Their, They're) going (to, too, two) begin construction as soon as the plans are finished.

26. We left (there, their, they're) house after the storm subsided.

27. I think (your, you're) going (to, too, two) win at least (to, too, two) more times.

28. The corporation moved (its, it's) home office.

Answering Multiple-Choice Questions on Grammar in Sentences

As you take the portion of the test that assesses your writing skills, apply what you know about the rules of grammar:

- Look for complete sentences.
- Check for endmarks, commas, and apostrophes.
- Look for subject-verb agreement and consistency in verb tense.
- Check the pronouns to make sure the correct form is used and that the number (singular or plural) is correct.
- Check those easily confused pairs of words.

ADDITIONAL RESOURCES

This has been a very fast review of only a few aspects of written English. For more help with these aspects and more, here are some books you can consult.

FOR NON-NATIVE SPEAKERS OF ENGLISH

- *English Made Simple* by Arthur Waldhorn and Arthur Ziegler (Made Simple Books)

- *Errors in English and How to Correct Them* by Harry Shaw (HarperCollins)
- *Living in English* by Betsy J. Blusser (National Textbook Company)

FOR EVERYONE

- *Better English* by Norman Lewis (Dell)
- *How to Improve Your Writing Skills in 20 Minutes a Day* by Judith Olson (LearningExpress, order information at the back of this book)
- *1001 Pitfalls in English Grammar* (Barron's)

ANSWERS

1. d.	**11.** works	**21.** he, me
2. a.	**12.** helps	**22.** he
3. d.	**13.** causes	**23.** It's, too, to
4. c.	**14.** Has	**24.** who
5. a.	**15.** a.	**25.** They're, to
6. a.	**16.** b.	**26.** their
7. c.	**17.** d.	**27.** you're, to, two
8. d.	**18.** his, he	**28.** its
9. b.	**19.** its	
10. takes	**20.** they	

C·H·A·P·T·E·R

WRITING

9

CHAPTER SUMMARY

This chapter gives vital help on writing an essay or a report for law enforcement exams, as well as on multiple-choice tests where you have to choose the most clearly written paragraph. Even if the exam you have to take doesn't test writing skills in these ways, your career as a law enforcement officer will require these skills.

 ost people would be stunned to learn that law enforcement officers spend up to a third of their duty time writing reports. Other professionals, such as lawyers and judges, base their actions and decisions on the data in these reports. Because of this, law enforcement candidates need solid writing skills.

KINDS OF WRITING QUESTIONS ON CIVIL SERVICE EXAMS

A civil service exam might test your writing skills in one of three ways:

- By asking you to write an essay from scratch
- By asking you to view a video (perhaps a dramatization of officers responding to a call) or listen to an interview, take notes, and write an incident report

- By asking you to choose from among several sentences the one that most clearly and accurately presents the facts

No matter which of the three methods is used, learning and applying a few basic principles will help you do well on this section of your test.

WRITING AN ESSAY

Your exam may actually have you write an essay not that different from the kinds of essays you might have written in school. This is the best way to tell whether you can use written language to express your ideas clearly. The most important thing to remember is to keep your writing simple and straightforward. You're writing to express yourself so that others can read and understand what you write. You're *not* writing to impress your high school English teacher. Use words most people will understand, and avoid long, drawn-out sentences that might confuse a reader.

CHOOSING A TOPIC

It's impossible to predict the questions, but chances are you'll be allowed to choose a general interest question most people could answer, such as:

- What events in your life caused you to choose law enforcement as a profession?
- Describe a person or event that has influenced your life.
- Describe a significant accomplishment in your life.
- Describe yourself.

Whatever the question, answer it by writing about something you know well. If you would enjoy having a conversation about the topic you're considering, it's probably a good choice.

Your time to write this essay will undoubtedly be limited. Start quickly and don't get too fancy. Starting is sometimes the hardest part, but if you begin with a thesis, you'll find writing much easier. A thesis is simply a sentence that *tells what the essay is about* and *forecasts how you will present your information.* The easiest way to write a thesis is to turn the question into a statement and add the main ideas. Take a look at these examples.

Question

How did you develop self-discipline?

Thesis

I learned self-discipline from taking music lessons and by caring for my younger siblings.

This thesis answers the question by suggesting the two ways the writer will present the information: writing about music lessons and writing about caring for siblings.

Question

Describe an event that taught you an important lesson.

Thesis

The car accident I had when I was 22 taught me that I was not immortal and that life is a precious gift.

This thesis tells specifically what the essay is going to be about—a car accident at age 22. It also forecasts how the writer will present the information: as a lesson about being mortal and as a lesson about the value of life. You may have noticed that the "question" isn't in the form of a question. That's common on tests.

Now try writing your own thesis statements for these two questions.

Question

Describe an event that taught you an important lesson.

Your Thesis

Question

How did you develop self-discipline?

Your Thesis

Do your thesis statements answer the question and forecast what your essay will cover? If so, you have written a thesis statement that will make the actual essay easier to write.

ORGANIZING YOUR IDEAS

The thesis establishes the destination and the direction for your essay; the essay will be easier to write when you know where you're going and how you're going to get there. Before you actually write the essay, take a few minutes to organize your thoughts and to make a quick outline. Choose two or three main ideas to write about in support of your thesis. Make a list of what you will write concerning each main idea. Once you've jotted down the ideas so you can see how they look, it's easier to consider the order. When you have to write an essay under timed testing conditions, it's best to begin with the strongest point first. Try to arrange the ideas in such a way that they can be easily hooked together, so your

essay will flow smoothly from one idea to another. This brief outline will make your essay easier to write.

Organize your ideas in paragraphs—units of thought that fully develop a single idea. Each paragraph should begin with a topic sentence that states the subject of the paragraph. The rest of the sentences in the paragraph should support, illustrate, or prove the topic sentence. These sentences can offer examples, narrate a sequence of events, explain an idea, or describe something.

WRITING THE ESSAY

You have a thesis, you have an outline, now all you need to do is write. Start with the topic sentence for your first paragraph, then follow it with several sentences that prove or develop the idea presented in the topic sentence.

Remember the purpose behind the essay. You're trying to show that you can **express** your ideas clearly. You're *not* out to impress anyone with your huge vocabulary or your ability to write long, involved, "intellectual-sounding" sentences. Just keep it simple. Write using complete sentences. Each sentence should present just one point in support of the topic sentence. If you keep your sentences short and specific, you're less likely to muddle your facts or make other mistakes that might distort the meaning or confuse the reader.

The topics you're given will most likely ask you to write about yourself. Use the "I, me" point of view as you write the essay to give it a natural, informal tone. The tone or attitude of your essay is important. You don't want your writing to be filled with slang or street language, but you don't want it to sound formal and stuffy either. It should sound like an educated person speaking in an informal situation, like a conversation. Think through each sentence before you write it. If it would sound awkward in a conversation, think of a way to rephrase the sentence before you write it.

Write using active verbs to make your essay more interesting. In a sentence with an active verb, the person or thing that performs the action is named before the verb, or the action word(s), in a sentence. The following examples illustrate the difference between active and passive verbs. The italicized words show who is performing the action. The underlined words are verbs.

Passive Verbs

I *was* taken to my first horse show by my *grandfather*.

I *was* taught to fish by my *mother* almost before *I was* taught to walk.

Active Verbs

My *grandfather* took me to my first horse show.

My *mother* taught me to fish almost before *I* learned to walk.

In each of the active verb sentences, the person performing the action is named first. If you look more closely at these examples, you'll notice that the active verb versions are shorter and clearer. They sound more like natural conversation. Strive for these qualities in your essay.

Finally, be concise and specific when you write. The best writing is that which clearly says the most using the fewest words. Avoid *general* statements that don't really say anything. Instead, write *specific* statements that give the reader a clear picture of what you have in mind. Detailed, *specific* language keeps readers interested and makes your ideas easier to remember. The following examples illustrate the difference.

General

My sister and I enjoyed each other's company as we were growing up. We had a lot of fun, and I will always remember her. We did interesting things and played fun games.

Specific

As children, my sister and I built rafts out of old barrels and tires, then tried to float them on the pond behind our house. I'll never forget playing war or hide-and-seek in the grove beside the pond.

The idea behind both of these versions is similar, but the specific example is more interesting and memorable. Be specific when you write.

Tips for Writing an Essay

- Keep it simple. Express, not impress.
- Start with a thesis. State the idea and forecast the direction.
- Organize first!
- Present ideas in paragraphs.
- Use the "I, me" point of view.
- Use active verbs.
- Be concise and specific.

Examine the sample question, thesis, and outline below to see this plan in action.

Question

Describe a well-known personality whom you admire.

Thesis

I admire Larry King because he is interesting to watch, because he handles controversial subjects well, and because he has staying power in a high-profile occupation.

I. Interesting to watch

   A. timely topics

   B. interesting guests

   C. humor

II. Handles controversial topics well

   A. straightforward and informative:

      doesn't gloss over tough issues

      doesn't "beat around the bush"

      probes for ideas behind opinions

   B. fair:

      tries to represent both sides of an issue equally

      steers callers and guests away from prejudicial assumptions

III. Staying power

   A. hasn't become sensational or extreme

   B. more impressed with his guests than with himself

   C. manages to stay fresh and enthusiastic night after night

Following the thesis in this essay, the writer would develop the essay in three paragraphs: one about how interesting Larry King is, one about how well he handles controversial issues, and one about the reasons behind his staying power as a media personality. The first sentence of each paragraph would be a complete sentence stating the main idea. Each subheading could be turned into a sentence supporting the topic sentence. The writer would give examples for each point.

You may want to write the essay outlined here for practice. Better yet, write your own thesis, outline, and essay about a personality you admire.

WRITING FROM VIDEO OR INTERVIEW NOTES

This kind of written exam most nearly represents the kind of writing law enforcement officers do in their jobs. You may see a video of officers responding to a call, or you may listen to a dramatization of an interview an officer might conduct. You'll be asked to take notes from which you'll write an incident report. This exercise tests your ability to record facts and events accurately and write about them clearly.

TAKING NOTES

Taking good notes is a vital first step. First, make sure you accurately record the most important information (who, what, when, where). Clearly identify the people involved and record all of the data the officers request: name, date of birth, address, age, etc. List every event, no matter how small or insignificant it may seem, in chronological order. If a time is mentioned, record the time next to the event.

When you write your report, you'll include "just the facts"—no conclusions, assumptions or predictions—so be sure to record specific data rather than the judgments you might make. For example, rather than writing, "violent suspect," record the specific behavior from which you drew that conclusion: "threw a bottle, knocked over a lamp and end table, said 'I'm gonna strangle you.'" Include as much specific detail as you can. Write clearly so you can decipher your notes later when it's time to write.

WRITING THE INCIDENT REPORT

The purpose of an incident report is to create a permanent record that clearly and accurately represents the facts. The same advice you read earlier about writing an essay applies to an incident report. Use plain English. Rather than trying to make your report sound "official" by writing jargon, use the ordinary language you would use in a conversation. Here, too, write short sentences with active verbs. Write in past tense (*asked, drove, went, escaped*) reporting action that has already happened. Keep your writing clear and crisp.

Begin with the most important information (who, what, when, where). Below are two versions of a beginning sentence. Which one is a better beginning for an incident report?

- On or approximately at 0335 hours on the date of February 5, 1996, Officer Barrett was dispatched to go to 628 Elm to investigate a noise disturbance complaint allegedly called in by one Andrea Jones, a resident at the above-stated address (date of birth January 18, 1971).
- At 3:35 a.m. on February 5, 1996, Officer Barrett arrived at 628 Elm and interviewed Andrea Jones (date of birth January 18, 1971), the resident who had called with a noise complaint.

If you chose the second option, you were correct. Although both sentences include identical information, the second one is shorter and easier to read. All of the

important data appears in the first line. The writer uses active verbs and avoids unnecessary words. On the other hand, the first option is long and difficult to read. It contains unnecessary words (*On or approximately at, the date of, go to*). The writer uses passive verbs (*was dispatched*) and jargon (*allegedly, above-stated address*) probably in an attempt to sound "official." The effect is to make the writing cumbersome and unclear. The report should begin with the most important information stated clearly and concisely.

After you've recorded the vital information, write about what happened in chronological order. Remember to keep your sentences and paragraphs clear and concise. Record only the facts, not your interpretations or assumptions, and write in such a way that others who read what you have written will draw the same conclusions you did. Don't state the conclusions for them; let the facts speak for themselves. Facts take longer to record than conclusions, but they are infinitely more valuable in an incident report. The examples below illustrate the difference.

Conclusion

Strader was drunk.

Facts

Strader smelled strongly of alcohol, slurred his words when he spoke, and stumbled often as he walked.

Tips for Writing from Notes

- Take thorough, accurate notes.
- Begin with the most important information first.
- Use plain English.
- Use active verbs in past tense.
- Report events in chronological order.
- Include just the facts, not conclusions or assumptions.

CHOOSING THE BEST OPTION

Your writing skills may be tested in yet another way. You may be asked to read two or more written versions of the same information and to choose the one that most clearly presents accurate information. Check for accuracy first. If the facts are wrong, the answer is wrong, no matter how well-written the answer choice is. If the facts are accurately represented in several of the answer choices, then you must evaluate the writing itself. Here are a few tips for choosing the **best** answer.

1. The **best** answer will be written in plain English in such a way that most readers can understand it the first time through. If you read through an answer choice and find you need to reread it to understand what it says, look for a better option.
2. The **best** option will present the information in logical order, usually chronological order. If the order seems questionable or is hard to follow, look for a better option.
3. The **best** option will be written with active rather than passive verbs. Answer choices written with

passive verbs sound formal and stuffy. Look for an option that sounds like normal conversation. Here's an example.

Passive Voice

At 8:25 p.m., Officer Sanchez was dispatched to 18 Grand, an apartment complex, where a burglary had been reported by Milo Andrews, the manager.

Active Voice

At 8:25 p.m., Officer Sanchez responded to a burglary reported by Milo Andrews, the manager of an apartment complex at 18 Grand.

The first version uses the passive verbs "was dispatched" and "had been reported" rather than active verbs. Example 2 uses the active verb "responded."

4. The **best** answer contains clearly identified pronouns (*he, she, him, her, them,* etc.) that match the number of nouns they represent. First, the pronouns should be clearly identified.

Unclear

Ann Dorr and the officer went to the precinct house, where she made her report.
Bob reminded his father that he had an appointment.

Clear

Ann Dorr and the officer went to the precinct house, where the officer made her report.
Bob reminded his father that Bob had an appointment.

An answer choice with clearly identified pronouns is a better choice than one with uncertain pronoun references. Sometimes the noun must be repeated to make the meaning clear.

In addition, the pronoun must match the noun it represents. If the noun is singular, the pronoun must be singular. Similarly, if the noun is plural, the pronoun must match.

Mismatch

I stopped the driver to tell them a headlight was burned out.

Match

I stopped the driver to tell him a headlight was burned out.

In the first example, *driver* is singular but the pronoun *them* is plural. In the second, the singular pronoun *him* matches the word it refers to.

5. The **best** option is one in which the verb tense is consistent. Look for answer choices that describe the action as though it has already happened, using past tense verbs (mostly -*ed* forms). The verb tense must remain consistent throughout the passage.

Inconsistent

I opened the trunk and find nothing unusual.

Consistent

I opened the trunk and found nothing unusual.

The verbs *opened* and *found* are both in the past tense in the second version. In the first, *find*, in the present tense, is inconsistent with *opened*.

6. The **best** option will use words clearly. Watch for unclear modifying words or phrases such as the ones in the following sentences. Misplaced and dangling modifiers can be hard to spot because your brain tries to make sense of things as it reads. In the case of misplaced or dangling modifiers, you may make a logical connection that is not present in the words.

Dangling Modifiers

Nailed to the tree, Cedric saw a "No Hunting" sign.
Waddling down the road, we saw a skunk.

Clear Modifiers

Cedric saw a "No Hunting" sign nailed to a tree.
We saw a skunk waddling down the road.

In the first version of the sentences, it sounds like *Cedric* was nailed to a tree and *we* were waddling down the road. The second version probably represents the writer's intentions: the *sign* was nailed to a tree and the *skunk* was waddling.

Misplaced Modifier

A dog followed the boy who was growling and barking.
George told us about safe sex in the kitchen.

Clear Modifiers

A dog who was growling and barking followed the boy.
In the kitchen, George told us about safe sex.

Do you think the boy was growling and barking? Did George discuss avoiding sharp knives and household poisons? The second version of each sentence represents the real situation.

7. Finally, the **best** option will use words efficiently. Avoid answer choices that are redundant (repeat unnecessarily) or wordy. Extra words take up valuable time and increase the chances that facts will be misunderstood. In the following examples, the italicized words are redundant or unnecessary. Try reading the sentences without the italicized words.

Redundant

They refunded our money *back to us.*

We can proceed *ahead* with the plan we made *ahead of time.*

The car was red *in color.*

Wordy

The reason he pursued the car *was* because it ran a stoplight.

We didn't know what *it was* we were doing.

There are many citizens *who* obey the law.

In each case, the sentence is simpler and easier to read without the italicized words. When you find an answer choice that uses unnecessary words, look for a better option.

The BEST Option:

- Is ACCURATE
- Is written in plain English
- Presents information in a logical order
- Uses active verbs
- Has clearly identified pronouns that match the number of the nouns they represent
- Has a consistent verb tense
- Uses words clearly
- Uses words efficiently

Here are four sample multiple-choice questions. By applying the principles explained in this section, choose the best version of each of the four sets of sentences. The answers and a short explanation for each question are at the end of the chapter.

1.

a. Vanover caught the ball. This was after it had been thrown by the shortstop. Vanover was the first baseman who caught the double-play ball. The shortstop was Hennings. He caught a line drive.

b. After the shortstop Hennings caught the line drive, he threw it to the first baseman Vanover for the double play.

c. After the line drive was caught by Hennings, the shortstop, it was thrown to Vanover at first base for a double play.

d. Vanover the first baseman caught the flip from shortstop Hennings.

2.

a. This writer attended the movie *Casino* starring Robert DeNiro.

b. The movie *Casino* starring Robert DeNiro was attended by me.

c. The movie *Casino* starring Robert DeNiro was attended by this writer.

d. I attended the movie *Casino* starring Robert DeNiro.

3.

    a. They gave cereal boxes with prizes inside to the children.

    b. They gave cereal boxes to children with prizes inside.

    c. Children were given boxes of cereal by them with prizes inside.

    d. Children were given boxes of cereal with prizes inside by them.

4.

    a. After playing an exciting drum solo, the crowd rose to its feet and then claps and yells until the band plays another cut from their new album.

    b. After playing an exciting drum solo, the crowd rose to its feet and then clapped and yelled until the band played another cut from their new album.

    c. After the drummer's exciting solo, the crowd rose to its feet and then claps and yells until the band plays another cut from their new album.

    d. After the drummer's exciting solo, the crowd rose to its feet and then clapped and yelled until the band played another cut from their new album.

Whether you write an essay yourself or choose the **best** option written by someone else, remember the basic principles of good writing. Use them in your writing and look for them in the writing you read.

ANSWERS

1. **b.** Answer **a** is unnecessarily wordy and the order is not logical. Answer **c** is written using passive voice verbs. Answer **d** omits a piece of important information.

2. **d.** Both Answers **a** and **c** use the stuffy-sounding *this writer.* Answer **d** is best because it uses an active verb.

3. **a.** In both Answers **b** and **c** the modifying phrase *with prizes inside* is misplaced. Both Answers **c** and **d** are written in passive rather than active voice.

4. **d.** Both Answers **a** and **b** contain a dangling modifier, stating that the crowd played an exciting drum solo. Both Answers **b** and **c** mix past and present verb tense. Only Answer **d** has clearly written modifiers and a consistent verb tense.

ADDITIONAL RESOURCES

This chapter has touched on only a few aspects of learning to write clearly. If you need more assistance to prepare for the exam, or if you want to improve your writing skills for your career, you might want additional help. Many high schools and community colleges offer inexpensive writing courses for adults in their continuing education departments, or you may be able to find a teacher who is willing to tutor you for a modest fee. In addition, you might consult one of the following books.

- *The Handbook of Good English* by Edward D. Johnson (Washington Square Press)
- *How to Improve Your Writing Skills in 20 Minutes a Day* by Judith Olson (LearningExpress, order information at the back of this book)
- *Smart English* by Anne Francis (Signet)
- *Writing Smart* by Marcia Lerner (Princeton Review)

C·H·A·P·T·E·R

VOCABULARY AND SPELLING

CHAPTER SUMMARY

Vocabulary and spelling are tested, at least indirectly, on most law enforcement exams. This chapter provides tips and exercises to help you improve your score in both areas.

A person's vocabulary is seen as a measure of an ability to express ideas clearly and precisely. Law enforcement officers must know the working vocabulary of the profession or have the tools for acquiring that vocabulary quickly. Spelling is regarded as a measure of a person's accuracy in presenting information. Law enforcement officers must be able to write correctly in order to communicate clearly. In addition, accurate spelling and a wide and flexible vocabulary are seen as the marks of thoughtful and well-educated people.

VOCABULARY

Many civil service exams test vocabulary. There are three basic kinds of questions.

- Synonyms and antonyms: Identifying words that mean the same or the opposite of given words

- Context: Determining the meaning of a word or phrase by noting how it is used in a sentence or paragraph
- Word parts: Choosing the meaning suggested by a part of the word, such as a prefix or suffix

SYNONYM AND ANTONYM QUESTIONS

A word is a *synonym* of another word if it has the same or nearly the same meaning as the other word. *Antonyms* are words with opposite meanings. Test questions often ask you to find the synonym or antonym of a word. If you're lucky, the word will be surrounded by a sentence that helps you guess what the word means. If you're less lucky, you'll just get the word, and then you have to figure out what the word means without any help.

Questions that ask for synonyms and antonyms can be tricky because they require you to recognize the meaning of several words that may be unfamiliar—not only the words in the questions but also the answer choices. Usually the best strategy is to *look* at the structure of the word and to *listen* for its sound. See if a part of a word looks familiar. Think of other words you know that have similar key elements. How could those words be related?

Synonym Practice

Try your hand at identifying the word parts and related words in these sample synonym questions. Circle the word that means the same or about the same as the underlined word. Answers and explanations appear right after the questions.

1. a set of <u>partial</u> prints
   a. identifiable
   b. incomplete
   c. visible
   d. enhanced

2. <u>substantial</u> evidence
   a. inconclusive
   b. weighty
   c. proven
   d. alleged

3. <u>corroborated</u> the statement
   a. confirmed
   b. negated
   c. denied
   d. challenged

4. <u>ambiguous</u> questions
   a. meaningless
   b. difficult
   c. simple
   d. vague

Answers to Synonym Questions

The explanations are just as important as the answers, because they show you how to go about choosing a synonym if you don't know the word.

1. **b.** *Partial* means *incomplete.* The key part of the word here is *part.* A partial print is only part of the whole.
2. **b.** *Substantial* evidence is *weighty.* The key part of the word here is *substance.* Substance has weight.
3. **a.** *Corroboration* is *confirmation.* The key part of the word here is the prefix *co-,* which means *with* or *together.* Corroboration means that one statement fits with another.
4. **d.** *Ambiguous* questions are *vague* or uncertain. The key part of this word is *ambi-,* which means *two* or *both.* An ambiguous question can be taken two ways.

Antonym Practice

The main danger in answering questions with antonyms is forgetting that you are looking for *opposites* rather than synonyms. Most questions will include one or more synonyms as answer choices. The trick is to keep your mind on the fact that you are looking for the opposite of the word. If you're allowed to mark in the books or on the test papers, circle the word *antonym* or *opposite* in the directions to help you remember.

Otherwise, the same tactics that work for synonym questions work for antonyms as well: try to determine the meaning of part of the word or to remember a context where you've seen the word before.

Circle the word that means the *opposite* of the underlined word in the sentences below. Answers are immediately after the questions.

5. zealous pursuit
   a. envious
   b. eager
   c. idle
   d. comical

6. inadvertently left
   a. mistakenly
   b. purposely
   c. cautiously
   d. carefully

7. exorbitant prices
   a. expensive
   b. unexpected
   c. reasonable
   d. outrageous

8. compatible workers
   a. comfortable
   b. competitive

   c. harmonious
   d. experienced

9. belligerent attitude
   a. hostile
   b. reasonable
   c. instinctive
   d. ungracious

Answers to Antonym Questions

Be sure to read the explanations as well as the right answers.

5. c. *Zealous* means *eager,* so *idle* is most nearly opposite. Maybe you've heard the word *zeal* before. One trick in this question is not to be misled by the similar sounds of *zealous* and *jealous.* The other is not to choose the synonym, *eager.*

6. b. *Inadvertently* means *by mistake,* so *purposely* is the antonym. The key element in this word is the prefix *in-,* which usually means *not, the opposite of.* As usual, one of the answer choices (a) is a synonym.

7. c. The key element here is *ex-,* which means *out of* or *away from. Exorbitant* literally means "out of orbit." The opposite of an *exorbitant* or *outrageous* price would be a *reasonable* one.

8. b. The opposite of *compatible* is *competitive.* Here you have to distinguish among three words that contain the same prefix, *com-,* and to let the process of elimination work for you. The other choices are too much like synonyms.

9. b. The key element in this word is the root *belli-,* which means *warlike.* The synonym choices, then, are *hostile* and *ungracious*; the antonym is *reasonable.*

CONTEXT QUESTIONS

Context is the surrounding text in which a word is used. Most people use context to help them determine the meaning of an unknown word. A vocabulary question that gives you a sentence around the vocabulary word is usually easier to answer than one with little or no context. The surrounding text can help you as you look for synonyms for the specified words in the sentences.

The best way to take meaning from context is to look for key words in sentences or paragraphs that convey the meaning of the text. If nothing else, the context will give you a means to eliminate wrong answer choices that clearly don't fit. The process of elimination will often leave you with the correct answer.

Context Practice

Try these sample questions. Circle the word that best describes the meaning of the underlined word in the sentence.

10. The members of the jury were <u>appalled</u> by the wild and uncontrolled behavior of the witness in the case.
    a. horrified
    b. amused
    c. surprised
    d. dismayed

11. Despite the fact that he appeared to have financial resources, the defendent claimed to be <u>destitute</u>.
    a. wealthy
    b. ambitious
    c. solvent
    d. impoverished

12. Though she was <u>distraught</u> over the disappearance of her child, the woman was calm enough to give the officer her description.
    a. punished
    b. distracted
    c. composed
    d. anguished

13. The unrepentant criminal expressed no <u>remorse</u> for his actions.
    a. sympathy
    b. regret
    c. reward
    d. complacency

Some tests may ask you to fill in the blank by choosing a word that fits the context. In the following questions, circle the word that best completes the sentence.

14. Professor Washington was a very_____ man known for his reputation as a scholar.
    a. stubborn
    b. erudite
    c. illiterate
    d. disciplined

15. His_____was demonstrated by his willingness to donate large amounts of money to worthy causes.
    a. honesty
    b. loyalty
    c. selfishness
    d. altruism

Answers to Context Questions

Check to see whether you were able to pick out the key words that help you define the target word, as well as whether you got the right answer.

10. a. The key words *wild* and *uncontrolled* signify *horror* rather than the milder emotions described by the other choices.

11. d. The key words here are *financial resources,* but this is a clue by contrast. The introductory *Despite the fact* signals that you should look for the opposite of the idea of having financial resources.

12. d. The key words here are *though* and *disappearance of her child,* signalling that you are looking for an opposite of *calm* in describing how the mother spoke to the officer. The only word strong enough to match the situation is *anguish.*

13. b. *Remorse* means *regret* for one's action. The part of the word here to beware of is the prefix *re-.* It doesn't signify anything in this word, though it often means *again* or *back.* Don't be confused by the two choices which also contain the prefix *re-.* The strategy here is to see which word sounds better in the sentence. The key words are *unrepentant* and *no,* indicating that you're looking for something that shows no repentance.

14. b. The key words here are *professor* and *scholarly.* Even if you don't know the word *erudite,* the other choices don't fit the description of the professor.

15. d. The key words here are *large amounts of money to worthy causes.* They give you a definition of the word you're looking for. Again, even if you don't know the word *altruism,* the other choices seem inappropriate to describe someone so generous.

For Non-Native Speakers of English

Be very careful not to be confused by the sound of words that may mislead you. Be sure you look at the word carefully, and pay attention to the structure and appearance of the word as well as its sound. You may be used to hearing English words spoken with an accent. The sounds of those words may be misleading in choosing a correct answer.

QUESTIONS ABOUT WORD PARTS

Some tests may ask you to find the meaning of a part of a word: roots, which are the main part of the word; prefixes, which go before the root word; or suffixes, which go after. Any of these elements can carry meaning or change the use of a word in a sentence. For instance, the suffix *-s* or *-es* can change the meaning of a noun from singular to plural: *boy, boys.* The prefix *un-* can change the meaning of a root word to its opposite: *necessary, unnecessary.*

To identify most parts of words, the best strategy is to think of words you already know which carry the same root, suffix, or prefix. Let what you know about those words help you to see the meaning in words that are less familiar.

Word Part Practice

Circle the word or phrase below that best describes the meaning of the underlined portion of the word. Answers appear after the questions.

16. <u>pro</u>active
    a. after
    b. forward
    c. toward
    d. behind

17. recession
  a. against
  b. see
  c. under
  d. back

18. contemporary
  a. with
  b. over
  c. apart
  d. time

19. etymology
  a. state of
  b. prior to
  c. study of
  d. quality of

20. vandalize
  a. to make happen
  b. to stop

  c. to fill
  d. to continue

Answers to Word Part Questions

Even if the word in the question was unfamiliar, you might have been able to guess the meaning of the prefix or suffix by thinking of some other word that has the same prefix or suffix.

16. b. Think of *propeller*. A propeller sends an airplane *forward*.
17. d. Think of *recall*: Manufacturers *recall* or *bring back* cars that are defective; people *recall* or *bring back* past events in memory.
18. a. Think of *congregation*: a group of people gather *with* each other in a house of worship.
19. c. Think of *biology*, the *study of* life.
20. a. Think of *scandalize*: to *make* something shocking *happen*.

WORDS THAT ARE EASILY CONFUSED

Vocabulary tests of any kind often contain words that are easily confused with each other. A smart test taker will be aware of these easily mixed up words or phrases:

accept: to receive willingly	**except:** exclude or leave out
complement: to complete	**compliment:** to say something flattering
council: a group that makes decisions	**counsel:** to give advice
contemptuous: having an attitude of contempt	**contemptible:** worthy of contempt
continuous: without interruption	**continual:** from time to time
emigrate: to move from	**immigrate:** to move to
ingenious: something clever	**ingenuous:** guileless or naive
oral: pertaining to the mouth	**verbal:** pertaining to language
persecute: to oppress someone	**prosecute:** to bring a legal action against someone

How to Answer Vocabulary Questions

- The key to answering vocabulary questions is to **notice and connect** what you do know to what you may not recognize.
- **Know your word parts.** You can recognize or make a good guess at the meanings of words when you see some suggested meaning in a root word, prefix, or suffix.
- **Note directions very carefully.** Remember when you are looking for opposites rather than synonyms.
- **Use a process of elimination.** Think of how the word makes sense in the sentence.
- **Don't be confused by words that sound like other words,** but may have no relation to the word you need.

A List of Word Parts

On the next page are some of the word elements seen most often in vocabulary tests. Simply reading them and their examples five to ten minutes a day will give you the quick recognition you need to make a good association with the meaning of an unfamiliar word.

SPELLING

Generally spelling tests are in a multiple-choice format. You will be given several possible spellings for a word and asked to identify the one that is correct. Thus, you must be able to see very fine differences between word spellings. The best way to prepare for a spelling test is to have a good grasp of the spelling fundamentals and be able to recognize when those rules don't apply.

Remember that English is full of exceptions in spelling. You have to develop a good eye to spot the errors.

Even though there are so many variant spellings for words in English, civil service tests generally are looking to make sure that you know and can apply the basic rules. Here are some of those rules to review:

- *i* before *e*, except after *c*, or when *ei* sounds like *a*
  Examples: piece, receive, neighbor
- *gh* can replace *f* or be silent
  Examples: enough, night
- Double the consonant when you add an ending
  Examples: forget/forgettable, shop/shopping
- Drop the *e* when you add *ing*
  Example: hope/hoping
- The spelling of prefixes and suffixes generally doesn't change
  Examples: project, propel, proactive

SPELLING PRACTICE

Here are some examples of how spelling would appear on a civil service test. Choose the word that is spelled correctly in the following sentences. This time there's no answer key. Instead, use your dictionary to find the right answers.

21. We went to an _____ of early Greek art.
- a. exibition
- b. exhibition
- c. excibition
- d. exebition

word element	meaning	example
ama	love	amateur
ambi	both	ambivalent, ambidextrous
aud	hear	audition
bell	war	belligerent, bellicose
bene	good	benefactor
cid/cis	cut	homicide, scissor
cogn/gno	know	knowledge, recognize
curr	run	current
flu/flux	flow	fluid, fluctuate
gress	to go	congress, congregation
in	not, in	ingenious
ject	throw	inject, reject
luc/lux	light	lucid, translucent
neo	new	neophyte
omni	all	omnivorous
pel/puls	push	impulse, propeller
pro	forward	project
pseudo	false	pseudonym
rog	ask	interrogate
sub	under	subjugate
spec/spic	look, see	spectator
super	over	superfluous
temp	time	contemporary, temporal
un	not, opposite	uncoordinated
viv	live	vivid

22. We will _____ go to the movies tonight.
   a. probly
   b. probbaly
   c. probely
   d. probably

23. We took _____ of pictures on our vacation.
   a. allot
   b. alot
   c. a lot
   d. alott

24. The high scorer had the greatest number of _____ answers.
   a. accurate
   b. acurate
   c. accuret
   d. acccurit

25. He was warned not to use _____ force.
   a. exessive
   b. excesive
   c. excessive
   d. excesive

USING SPELLING LISTS

Some test makers will give you a list to study before you take the test. If you have a list to work with, here are some suggestions.

- Divide the list into groups of three, five, or seven to study. Consider making flash cards of the words you don't know.
- Highlight or circle the tricky elements in each word.
- Cross out or discard any words that you already know for certain. Don't let them get in the way of the ones you need to study.
- Say the words as you read them. Spell them out in your mind so you can "hear" the spelling.

Here's a sample spelling list. These words are typical of the words that appear on exams. If you aren't given a list by the agency that's testing you, study this one.

achievement	doubtful	ninety
allege	eligible	noticeable
anxiety	enough	occasionally
appreciate	enthusiasm	occurred
asthma	equipped	offense
arraignment	exception	official
autonomous	fascinate	pamphlet
auxiliary	fatigue	parallel
brief	forfeit	personnel
ballistics	gauge	physician
barricade	grieve	politics
beauty	guilt	possess
beige	guarantee	privilege
business	harass	psychology
bureau	hazard	recommend
calm	height	referral
cashier	incident	recidivism
capacity	indict	salary
cancel	initial	schedule
circuit	innocent	seize
colonel	irreverent	separate
comparatively	jeopardy	specific
courteous	knowledge	statute
criticism	leisure	surveillance
custody	license	suspicious
cyclical	lieutenant	tentative
debt	maintenance	thorough
definitely	mathematics	transferred
descend	mortgage	warrant

How to Answer Spelling Questions

- **Sound out the word in your mind.** Remember that long vowels inside words usually are followed by single consonants: *sofa, total.* Short vowels inside words usually are followed by double consonants: *dribble, scissors.*
- **Give yourself auditory (listening) clues when you learn words.** Say *"Wed-nes-day"* or *"lis-ten"* or *"bus-i-ness"* to yourself so that you remember to add letters you do not hear.
- **Look at each part of a word.** See if there is a root, prefix or suffix that will always be spelled the same way. For example, in *uninhabitable, un-, in-,* and *-able* are always spelled the same. What's left is *habit,* a self-contained root word that's pretty easy to spell.

MORE PRACTICE IN VOCABULARY AND SPELLING

Here is a second set of practice exercises with samples of each kind of question covered in this chapter. Answers to all questions except spelling questions are at the end of the chapter. For spelling questions, use a dictionary.

Circle the word that means the same or nearly the same as the underlined word.

26. convivial company
    a. lively
    b. dull
    c. tiresome
    d. dreary

27. conspicuous behavior
    a. secret
    b. notable
    c. visible
    d. boorish

28. meticulous record-keeping
    a. dishonest
    b. casual
    c. painstaking
    d. careless

29. superficial wounds
    a. life-threatening
    b. bloody
    c. severe
    d. shallow

30. impulsive actions
    a. cautious
    b. imprudent
    c. courageous
    d. cowardly

Circle the word that is most nearly opposite in meaning to the underlined word.

31. amateur athlete
    a. professional
    b. successful
    c. unrivaled
    d. former

32. lucid opinions
    a. clear
    b. strong
    c. hazy
    d. heartfelt

33. traveling <u>incognito</u>
   a. unrecognized
   b. alone
   c. by night
   d. publicly

34. <u>incisive</u> reporting
   a. mild
   b. sharp
   c. dangerous
   d. insightful

35. <u>tactful</u> comments
   a. rude
   b. pleasant
   c. complimentary
   d. sociable

Using the context, choose the word that means the same or nearly the same as the underlined word.

36. Though he had little time, the student took <u>copious</u> notes in preparation for the test.
   a. limited
   b. plentiful
   c. illegible
   d. careless

37. Though flexible about homework, the teacher was <u>adamant</u> that papers be in on time.
   a. liberal
   b. casual
   c. strict
   d. pliable

38. The condition of the room after the party was <u>deplorable</u>.
   a. regrettable
   b. pristine
   c. festive
   d. tidy

Choose the word that best completes the following sentences.

39. Her position as a(n) _____ teacher took her all over the city.
   a. primary
   b. secondary
   c. itinerant
   d. permanent

40. Despite her promise to stay in touch, she remained _____ and difficult to locate.
   a. steadfast
   b. stubborn
   c. dishonest
   d. elusive

Choose the word or phrase closest in meaning to the underlined part of the word.

41. <u>uni</u>verse
   a. one
   b. three
   c. under
   d. opposite

42. <u>re</u>entry
  a. back
  b. push
  c. against
  d. forward

43. <u>bene</u>fit
  a. bad
  b. suitable
  c. beauty
  d. good

44. educat<u>ion</u>
  a. something like
  b. state of
  c. to increase
  d. unlike

45. urban<u>ite</u>
  a. resident of
  b. relating to
  c. that which is
  d. possessing

Circle the correct spelling of the word that fits in the blank.

46. The information was _____
to the action.
  a. irelevent
  b. irrevelent
  c. irrelevant
  d. irrevelent

47. He made no _____ to take
the job.
  a. comittment
  b. commitment
  c. comitment
  d. comittmint

48. He made an income _____
to meet his needs.
  a. adaquate
  b. adequate
  c. adiquate
  d. adequet

49. We went to eat at a fancy new _____.
  a. restarant
  b. restaraunt
  c. restaurant
  d. resteraunt

50. The vote was _____ to elect
the chairman.
  a. unannimous
  b. unanimous
  c. unanimus
  d. unaminous

ADDITIONAL RESOURCES

One of the best resources for any adult student is the public library. Many libraries have sections for adult learners or for those preparing to enter or change careers. Those sections contain skill books and review books on a number of subjects, including spelling and vocabulary. Here are some books you might consult:

- *504 Absolutely Essential Words* by Murray Bromberg et al. (Barron's)
- *All About Words: An Adult Approach to Vocabulary Building* by Maxwell Nurnberg and Morris Rosenblum (Mentor Books)
- *Checklists for Vocabulary Study* by Richard Yorkey (Longman)

- *Vocabulary and Spelling in 20 Minutes a Day* by Judith Meyers (LearningExpress, order information at the back of this book)
- *Word Watcher's Handbook* by Phyllis Martin (St. Martin's)
- *Spelling Made Simple* by Stephen V. Ross (Doubleday)
- *Spelling the Easy Way* by Joseph Mersand and Francis Griffith (Barron's)
- *Word Smart Revised* by Adam Robinson (The Princeton Review)

ANSWERS TO PRACTICE QUESTIONS

26. a.
27. c.
28. c.
29. d.
30. b.
31. a.
32. c.

33. d.
34. a.
35. a.
36. b.
37. c.
38. a.
39. c.

40. d.
41. a.
42. a.
43. d.
44. b.
45. a.

C·H·A·P·T·E·R 11

CALIFORNIA STATE POLICE EXAM 2

CHAPTER SUMMARY

This chapter presents a second exam based on the test written by the California Peace Officer Standards and Training (POST) Commission and used to assess applicants to the California Highway Patrol. After working through the material in the preceding chapters on various kinds of exam questions, take this exam to see how much you've improved since you took the first test.

T he test that follows, like the first practice test, is modeled on the California POST Commission's reading and writing exam for entry-level law enforcement personnel. This test is the one the California Highway Patrol uses to screen applicants for the position of State Traffic Officer.

Book One of this test covers clarity of expression (grammar), vocabulary, spelling, and reading comprehension. Book Two is a different kind of reading test where you have to fill in the missing words in a passage. If you haven't read the section in Chapter 7 on answering fill-in-the-blank reading questions, do it now, before you take the test.

You have two and a half hours to answer the 105 questions on this test. Book One has 65 multiple-choice questions, and Book Two has 20 answer blanks in each of two reading passages for a total of 40 questions. Allow yourself only those two and a half hours to take this test. Remember what you learned about timing and pacing in Chapter 5 of this book, so you'll be able to get through the test in that amount of time.

The answer sheet for the test is on the next page, and the test comes right after. At the end of the test is an answer key, including explanations for clarity and reading questions. If you need to know why a vocabu-lary or spelling answer is correct, use a dictionary. After the key is a scoring guide. But remember, this is a learning experience and not the real exam. You should use this test to help you understand how the test works—which means that the explanations of the answers are as important as the test itself.

BOOK ONE

1.	ⓐ	ⓑ	ⓒ	ⓓ	23.	ⓐ	ⓑ	ⓒ	ⓓ	45.	ⓐ	ⓑ	ⓒ	ⓓ
2.	ⓐ	ⓑ	ⓒ	ⓓ	24.	ⓐ	ⓑ	ⓒ	ⓓ	46.	ⓐ	ⓑ	ⓒ	ⓓ
3.	ⓐ	ⓑ	ⓒ	ⓓ	25.	ⓐ	ⓑ	ⓒ	ⓓ	47.	ⓐ	ⓑ	ⓒ	ⓓ
4.	ⓐ	ⓑ	ⓒ	ⓓ	26.	ⓐ	ⓑ	ⓒ	ⓓ	48.	ⓐ	ⓑ	ⓒ	ⓓ
5.	ⓐ	ⓑ	ⓒ	ⓓ	27.	ⓐ	ⓑ	ⓒ	ⓓ	49.	ⓐ	ⓑ	ⓒ	ⓓ
6.	ⓐ	ⓑ	ⓒ	ⓓ	28.	ⓐ	ⓑ	ⓒ	ⓓ	50.	ⓐ	ⓑ	ⓒ	ⓓ
7.	ⓐ	ⓑ	ⓒ	ⓓ	29.	ⓐ	ⓑ	ⓒ	ⓓ	51.	ⓐ	ⓑ	ⓒ	ⓓ
8.	ⓐ	ⓑ	ⓒ	ⓓ	30.	ⓐ	ⓑ	ⓒ	ⓓ	52.	ⓐ	ⓑ	ⓒ	ⓓ
9.	ⓐ	ⓑ	ⓒ	ⓓ	31.	ⓐ	ⓑ	ⓒ	ⓓ	53.	ⓐ	ⓑ	ⓒ	ⓓ
10.	ⓐ	ⓑ	ⓒ	ⓓ	32.	ⓐ	ⓑ	ⓒ	ⓓ	54.	ⓐ	ⓑ	ⓒ	ⓓ
11.	ⓐ	ⓑ	ⓒ	ⓓ	33.	ⓐ	ⓑ	ⓒ	ⓓ	55.	ⓐ	ⓑ	ⓒ	ⓓ
12.	ⓐ	ⓑ	ⓒ	ⓓ	34.	ⓐ	ⓑ	ⓒ	ⓓ	56.	ⓐ	ⓑ	ⓒ	ⓓ
13.	ⓐ	ⓑ	ⓒ	ⓓ	35.	ⓐ	ⓑ	ⓒ	ⓓ	57.	ⓐ	ⓑ	ⓒ	ⓓ
14.	ⓐ	ⓑ	ⓒ	ⓓ	36.	ⓐ	ⓑ	ⓒ	ⓓ	58.	ⓐ	ⓑ	ⓒ	ⓓ
15.	ⓐ	ⓑ	ⓒ	ⓓ	37.	ⓐ	ⓑ	ⓒ	ⓓ	59.	ⓐ	ⓑ	ⓒ	ⓓ
16.	ⓐ	ⓑ	ⓒ	ⓓ	38.	ⓐ	ⓑ	ⓒ	ⓓ	60.	ⓐ	ⓑ	ⓒ	ⓓ
17.	ⓐ	ⓑ	ⓒ	ⓓ	39.	ⓐ	ⓑ	ⓒ	ⓓ	61.	ⓐ	ⓑ	ⓒ	ⓓ
18.	ⓐ	ⓑ	ⓒ	ⓓ	40.	ⓐ	ⓑ	ⓒ	ⓓ	62.	ⓐ	ⓑ	ⓒ	ⓓ
19.	ⓐ	ⓑ	ⓒ	ⓓ	41.	ⓐ	ⓑ	ⓒ	ⓓ	63.	ⓐ	ⓑ	ⓒ	ⓓ
20.	ⓐ	ⓑ	ⓒ	ⓓ	42.	ⓐ	ⓑ	ⓒ	ⓓ	64.	ⓐ	ⓑ	ⓒ	ⓓ
21.	ⓐ	ⓑ	ⓒ	ⓓ	43.	ⓐ	ⓑ	ⓒ	ⓓ	65.	ⓐ	ⓑ	ⓒ	ⓓ
22.	ⓐ	ⓑ	ⓒ	ⓓ	44.	ⓐ	ⓑ	ⓒ	ⓓ					

BOOK TWO

WRITE 1ST LETTER OF WORD HERE

CODE LETTERS HERE

| 1 | 2 | 3 | 4 | 5 | 6 | 7 | 8 | 9 | 10 |

A B C D E F G H I J K L M N O P Q R S T U V W X Y Z

| 11 | 12 | 13 | 14 | 15 | 16 | 17 | 18 | 19 | 20 |

A B C D E F G H I J K L M N O P Q R S T U V W X Y Z

| 21 | 22 | 23 | 24 | 25 | 26 | 27 | 28 | 29 | 30 |

A B C D E F G H I J K L M N O P Q R S T U V W X Y Z

| 31 | 32 | 33 | 34 | 35 | 36 | 37 | 38 | 39 | 40 |

A B C D E F G H I J K L M N O P Q R S T U V W X Y Z

CALIFORNIA STATE POLICE EXAM 2
BOOK 1

PART ONE: CLARITY

In the following sets of sentences, choose the sentence that is most clearly written.

1.
a. They finished their search, left the building, and return to police headquarters.
b. They finished their search, left the building, and returns to police headquarters.
c. They finished their search, left the building, and returned to police headquarters.
d. They finished their search, left the building, and returning to police headquarters.

2.
a. When her workday is over, Officer Hernandez likes to watch TV, preferring sitcoms to police dramas.
b. When her workday is over. Officer Hernandez likes to watch TV, preferring sitcoms to police dramas.
c. When her workday is over, Officer Hernandez likes to watch TV. Preferring sitcoms to police dramas.
d. When her workday is over, Officer Hernandez likes to watch TV, preferring sitcoms. To police dramas.

3.
a. Officer Chen thought they should call for backup; moreover, Officer Jovanovich disagreed.
b. Officer Chen thought they should call for backup; meanwhile, Officer Jovanovich disagreed.
c. Officer Chen thought they should call for backup; however, Officer Jovanovich disagreed.
d. Officer Chen thought they should call for backup; furthermore, Officer Jovanovich disagreed.

4.
a. Corky and Moe, respected members of the K-9 Corps, has sniffed out every ounce of cocaine in the warehouse.
b. Corky and Moe, respected members of the K-9 Corps, sniffs out every ounce of cocaine in the warehouse.
c. Corky and Moe, respected members of the K-9 Corps, sniffing out every ounce of cocaine in the warehouse.
d. Corky and Moe, respected members of the K-9 Corps, sniffed out every ounce of cocaine in the warehouse.

5.

a. When ordered to be removing their jewelry and lying down on the floor, not a single bank customer resisted.

b. When ordered to have removed their jewelry and to have lain down on the floor, not a single bank customer resisted.

c. When ordered to remove their jewelry and lie down on the floor, not a single bank customer resisted.

d. When ordered to remove their jewelry and be lying down on the floor, not a single bank customer resisted.

6.

a. The evidence had been improperly gathered, the case was dismissed.

b. Because the evidence had been improperly gathered, the case was dismissed.

c. Because the evidence had been improperly gathered. The case was dismissed.

d. The evidence had been improperly gathered the case was dismissed.

7.

a. A police officer can expect danger when you respond to a domestic dispute.

b. A police officer can expect danger when one responds to a domestic dispute.

c. A police officer can expect danger when responding to a domestic dispute.

d. A police officer can expect danger when we respond to a domestic dispute.

8.

a. Once the investigation begins, and there will be no turning back.

b. Once the investigation begins, there will be no turning back.

c. Once the investigation begins, so there will be no turning back.

d. Once the investigation begins, thus there will be no turning back.

9.

a. Officer DeAngelo phoned his partner every day when he was in the hospital.

b. When his partner was in the hospital, Officer DeAngelo phoned him every day.

c. When in the hospital, a phone call was made every day by Officer DeAngelo to his partner.

d. His partner received a phone call from Officer DeAngelo every day while he was in the hospital.

10.

a. Some of the case transcripts I have to type are very long, but that doesn't bother one if the cases are interesting.

b. Some of the case transcripts I have to type are very long, but that doesn't bother you if the cases are interesting.

c. Some of the case transcripts I have to type are very long, but it doesn't bother a person if the cases are interesting.

d. Some of the case transcripts I have to type are very long, but that doesn't bother me if the cases are interesting.

11.

a. Lieutenant Jenny Crabtree, along with one of her coworkers, has written a pamphlet about public safety.

b. Lieutenant Jenny Crabtree, along with one of her coworkers, have written a pamphlet about public safety.

c. Lieutenant Jenny Crabtree and one of her coworkers has written a pamphlet about public safety.

d. Lieutenant Jenny Crabtree have written a pamphlet about public safety with one of her coworkers.

12.

a. When not on duty, Officer Mike O'Rourke enjoys attending cooking class. Where he recently learned how to make an excellent soufflé.

b. When not on duty, Officer Mike O'Rourke enjoys attending cooking class, where he recently learned how to make an excellent soufflé.

c. Officer Mike O'Rourke enjoys attending cooking class. Where, when not on duty, he recently learned how to make an excellent soufflé.

d. When not on duty. Mike O'Rourke enjoys attending cooking class, where he recently learned how to make an excellent soufflé.

13.

a. Some people believe that "you can't legislate morality"; moreover, it's done every day.

b. Some people believe that "you can't legislate morality"; secondly, it's done every day.

c. Some people believe that "you can't legislate morality"; in addition, it's done every day.

d. Some people believe that "you can't legislate morality"; however, it's done every day.

14.

a. There is no true relationship between ethics and the law.

b. Ethics and the law having no true relationship.

c. Between ethics and the law, no true relationship.

d. Ethics and the law is no true relationship.

15.

a. Before he realized it, he had drunken the entire bottle of schnapps.

b. Before he realized it, he had drank the entire bottle of schnapps.

c. Before he realized it, he had drinked the entire bottle of schnapps.

d. Before he realized it, he had drunk the entire bottle of schnapps.

PART TWO: VOCABULARY

In each of the following sentences, choose the word or phrase that most nearly expresses the same meaning as the underlined word.

16. The general public was <u>apathetic</u> about the verdict.
    a. enraged
    b. indifferent
    c. suspicious
    d. saddened

17. The theories of some criminal psychologists were <u>fortified</u> by the new research.
    a. reinforced
    b. altered
    c. disputed
    d. developed

18. One of the duties of a captain is to <u>delegate</u> responsibility.
    a. analyze
    b. respect
    c. criticize
    d. assign

19. The lecture about prison overcrowding <u>aroused</u> many audience members.
    a. informed
    b. disappointed
    c. provoked
    d. deceived

20. The police department building was an <u>expansive</u> facility.
    a. obsolete
    b. meager
    c. spacious
    d. costly

21. Two inmates were involved in an <u>animated</u> conversation.
    a. abbreviated
    b. civil
    c. secret
    d. lively

22. The residents of that area were considered to be <u>compliant</u> in regard to the seat belt law.
    a. skeptical
    b. obedient
    c. forgetful
    d. appreciative

23. Following the disturbance, town officials felt the need to <u>augment</u> the laws pertaining to mass demonstrations.
    a. repeal
    b. evaluate
    c. expand
    d. criticize

24. Although Marty Albertson's after-hours security job was regarded by many as <u>menial</u>, he liked the peace and solitude it offered.
    a. lowly
    b. boring
    c. unpleasant
    d. unrewarding

25. Although the police might be able to help Mr. Chen recover his stolen property, he <u>obstinately</u> refuses to file a complaint.
  a. repeatedly
  b. reluctantly
  c. foolishly
  d. stubbornly

26. For all the problems faced by his district, Congressman Owly regarded budget cuts as a <u>panacea</u>.
  a. cure
  b. result
  c. cause
  d. necessity

27. The attorney's <u>glib</u> remarks irritated the judge.
  a. angry
  b. superficial
  c. insulting
  d. dishonest

28. On the witness stand, the suspect, who was accused of several murders, appeared <u>nondescript</u>.
  a. lethargic
  b. undistinguished
  c. respectable
  d. impeccable

29. When the Bakaras heard that a drug dealer had moved in next door, they were <u>incredulous</u>.
  a. fearful
  b. outraged
  c. disbelieving
  d. inconsolable

30. The police department recruited Officer Long because she was <u>proficient</u> in the use of computers to track down deadbeats.
  a. experienced
  b. unequaled
  c. efficient
  d. skilled

PART THREE: SPELLING

In each of the following sentences, choose the correct spelling of the missing word.

31. The tip came from an _____ source.
  a. anynonimous
  b. anonimous
  c. anounymous
  d. anonymous

32. The officers brought back an _____ amount of evidence.
  a. extraordinary
  b. extraordinery
  c. extrordinary
  d. ecstraordinary

33. The investigator gave his _____ that the report would be completed on time.
  a. asurrance
  b. assurance
  c. assurence
  d. assureance

34. The purpose of the law was debated
_____.
a. frequently
b. frequintly
c. frequentlly
d. frequentley

35. The _____ was placed on scientific
evidence.
a. enphasis
b. emphisis
c. emphasis
d. emfasis

36. When officers arrived, the victim was in a
_____ state.
a. delirious
b. dilerious
c. delireous
d. delirous

37. Each of the new officers had the same
_____.
a. asspiration
b. asparation
c. aspirration
d. aspiration

38. The young man wished to _____ his
right to speak with an attorney.
a. excercise
b. exercise
c. exersize
d. exercize

39. The veteran officer and the rookie were a
_____ pair.
a. compattible
b. compatable
c. compatible
d. commpatible

40. In many states, road tests require
_____ parking.
a. paralel
b. paralell
c. parallal
d. parallel

41. The paramedics attempted to _____
the victim.
a. stabilize
b. stablize
c. stableize
d. stableise

42. Prosecutors argued that testimony concerning
the past behavior of the accused was
_____.
a. irelevent
b. irelevant
c. irrelevant
d. irrelevent

43. The mayor pointed to the _____ crime
rate statistics.
a. encouredging
b. encouraging
c. incurraging
d. incouraging

44. The patient will have a _____ hearing on Friday.
    a. commitment
    b. committment
    c. comittment
    d. comitment

45. The prisoner's alibi seemed _____ on the face of it.
    a. rediculous
    b. rediculus
    c. ridiculous
    d. ridiculus

PART FOUR: READING COMPREHENSION

Several reading passages, each accompanied by three or more questions, follow. Answer each question based on what is stated or implied in the preceding passage.

The rules for obtaining evidence, set down in state and federal law, usually come to our attention when they work to the advantage of defendants in court, but these laws were not created with the courtroom in mind. They were formulated with the pragmatic intent of shaping police procedure before the arrest, in order to ensure justice, thoroughness, and the preservation of civil liberties. A good police officer must be as well schooled in the rules for properly obtaining evidence as is a defense lawyer or risk losing a conviction. When a case is thrown out of court or a defendant is released because of these evidentiary "technicalities," we are often angered and mystified, but we are not always aware of how these rules of evidence shape police procedure in positive ways every day.

46. The main idea of this passage is that
    a. the rules of evidence protect the rights of defendants at trial
    b. police officers should know the rules of evidence
    c. rules of evidence help shape police procedure
    d. the rules of evidence have more positive than negative effects

47. According to the passage, rules of evidence are designed to ensure all of the following EXCEPT
    a. meticulousness in gathering evidence
    b. proof of guilt
    c. protection of individual rights
    d. fairness of treatment

48. According to the passage, why should a police officer know the rules of evidence?
    a. The rules protect the rights of the accused.
    b. The public does not appreciate the rules' importance.
    c. An officer must follow the rules to obtain a conviction.
    d. Following the rules protects officers from accusations of misconduct.

49. In saying that the intent of rules of evidence is "pragmatic," the author most likely means that
   a. the focus of the rules is on police procedures in the field rather than on legal maneuvers in court
   b. the practical nature of the rules enables lawyers to use them in court to protect defendants
   c. the framers of these rules designed them to maintain idealistic standards of fairness
   d. the rules are often misused in court because of their limited scope

Stalking—the "willful, malicious, and repeated following and harassing of another person"—is probably as old as human society. But in the United States, until 1990, no substantive law existed to protect the stalking victim. The most that police officials could do was arrest the stalker for a minor offense or suggest the victim obtain a restraining order, a civil remedy often ignored by the offender. (One of the Orange County victims mentioned below was shot by her husband while carrying a restraining order in her purse.) Frightened victims had their worst fears confirmed: They would have to be harmed—or killed—before anything could be done.

In 1990, however, partly because of the 1989 stalker-murder of television star Rebecca Schaeffer, and partly because of the 1990 stalker-murders of four Orange County women in a single six-week period, California drafted the first anti-stalking law. Now most states have similar laws.

The solution is not perfect: Some stalkers are too mentally deranged or obsessed to fear a prison term. There is danger, however small, of abuse of the law, particularly in marital disputes. Most importantly, both police and society need better education about stalk-

ing, especially about its often sexist underpinnings. (The majority of stalking victims are women terrorized by former husbands or lovers.)

But the laws are a start, carrying with them felony penalties of up to ten years in prison for those who would attempt to control or possess others through intimidation and terror.

50. Which of the following best expresses the main idea of the passage?
   a. More education is needed about sexism, as it is the most important element in the crime of stalking.
   b. Stalking is thought of as a new kind of crime, but it has probably existed throughout human history.
   c. The new anti-stalking legislation is an important weapon against the crime of stalking, though it is not the complete answer.
   d. Today almost every state in the U.S. has an effective, if not perfect, anti-stalking law.

51. Based on the passage, which of the following is likely the most common question asked of police by stalking victims prior to 1990?
   a. How can I get a restraining order?
   b. Does he have to hurt me before you'll arrest him?
   c. Why is this person stalking me?
   d. Is it legal for me to carry a weapon in my purse?

52. Which of the following is NOT mentioned in the passage as a weakness in the new anti-stalking legislation?
   a. The laws alone might not deter some stalkers.
   b. A person might be wrongly accused of being a stalker.
   c. Neither the police nor the public completely understand the crime.
   d. Victims do not yet have adequate knowledge about anti-stalking laws.

53. Based on the passage, which of the following is the main reason restraining orders are ineffective in preventing stalking?
   a. No criminal charges can be leveled against the violator.
   b. Until 1990, restraining orders could not be issued against stalkers.
   c. Law enforcement officials do not take such orders seriously.
   d. Restraining orders apply only to married couples.

54. Based on the information in the passage, which of the following did the murders of Rebecca Schaeffer and the Orange County woman mentioned in the first paragraph have in common?
   a. Both murders provided impetus for anti-stalking laws.
   b. Both victims sought, but could not obtain, legal protection.
   c. Both victims were stalked and killed by a husband or lover.
   d. Both murders were the result of sexism.

55. Which of the following is NOT a stated or implied motive for stalking?
   a. to own the victim
   b. to terrify the victim
   c. to rob the victim
   d. to badger the victim

Law enforcement officers must read suspects their Miranda rights upon taking them into custody. When a suspect who is merely being questioned incriminates himself, he might later claim to have been in custody, and seek to have the case dismissed on the grounds of having been unapprised of his Miranda rights. In such cases, a judge must make a determination as to whether or not a reasonable person would have believed himself to have been in custody, based on certain criteria. The judge must determine whether the suspect was questioned in a threatening manner (for example, if the suspect was seated while the law enforcement officer remained standing) and whether the suspect was aware that he or she was free to leave at any time. Officers must be aware of these criteria and take care not to give suspects grounds for later claiming they believed themselves to be in custody.

56. What is the main idea of the passage?
   a. Law enforcement officers must remember to read suspects their Miranda rights.
   b. Judges, not law enforcement officers, make the final determination as to whether or not a suspect was in custody.
   c. Law enforcement officers who are merely questioning a suspect must not give the suspect the impression that he or she is in custody.
   d. Miranda rights needn't be read to all suspects before questioning.

57. When is a suspect not in custody?
   a. when free to refuse to answer questions
   b. when free to leave the station
   c. when apprised of his or her Miranda rights
   d. when not apprised of his or her Miranda rights

58. When must law enforcement officers read Miranda rights to a suspect?
   a. while questioning the suspect
   b. before taking the suspect to the station
   c. while placing the suspect under arrest
   d. before releasing the suspect

59. An officer who is questioning a suspect who is not under arrest must
   a. read the suspect his Miranda rights
   b. inform the suspect that he is free to leave
   c. advise the suspect of his right to a lawyer
   d. allow the suspect a phone call

At 8:16 a.m., a police operator received a report of an accident on Morton Avenue near Farley Street from Helen Moreno of 1523 Morton Avenue. The caller said she had just arrived home when she heard the collision from her living room. Officer Rayburn arrived on the scene at 8:19. He saw that three vehicles, including an armored truck, were involved and that the driver of the green sedan was unconscious. He called for an ambulance and backup. He then checked the injured driver, saw that he was not bleeding, and covered him with a blanket provided by Mrs. Moreno. Martin Wilcox, of 1526 Morton, who was a passenger in the green sedan, identified the driver as Henry Woolf, also of 1526 Morton. Mrs. Moreno identified the third vehicle involved in the accident, a blue convertible, as her car. The ambulance arrived at 8:24. At 8:25, four officers, including Lieutenant Watts, arrived. Lieutenant

Watts assigned Officers Rayburn and Stein to blocking off both streets and controlling traffic, Officer Washington to security on the armored truck, and Officer Parisi to examination of the skid marks on Farley Street. Mr. Wilcox told Lieutenant Watts that Woolf had stopped at the "T" intersection, then turned left onto Morton. Wilcox said the driver's side was struck almost immediately by the truck, which was skidding down Morton. The impact caused the Woolf vehicle to strike Mrs. Moreno's convertible. Frank Burroughs, the driver of the armored truck, told Officer Washington that he was due at Security Bank at 8:10 and that his brakes had failed. After checking with Lieutenant Watts and Officer Parisi, Officer Washington cited Burroughs for speeding, failing to obey a stop sign, and giving false information.

60. Who was the first person to view the accident scene?
   a. Lieutenant Watts
   b. Officer Washington
   c. Officer Rayburn
   d. the police operator

61. Which of the following can be concluded about the Morton Avenue-Farley Street intersection?
   a. There were at least two stop signs there.
   b. Farley Street is a one-way street.
   c. Morton Avenue runs north and south.
   d. No cars were parked near the intersection.

62. Which of the following best represents the order in which the accident occurred?

a. The Woolf vehicle struck the Moreno vehicle, which struck the armored vehicle.

b. The armored vehicle struck the Woolf vehicle, which struck the Moreno vehicle.

c. The Moreno vehicle struck the armored vehicle, which struck the Woolf vehicle.

d. The armored vehicle struck the Moreno vehicle, which struck the Woolf vehicle.

63. Who examined evidence relating to Frank Burroughs' claim that his brakes failed?

a. Officer Rayburn

b. Officer Stein

c. Officer Washington

d. Officer Parisi

64. Which vehicle had been traveling on Farley Street?

a. the green sedan

b. the blue convertible

c. the armored truck

d. the ambulance

65. Which of the following can be concluded about Helen Moreno's vehicle?

a. It was parked on a steep incline.

b. It was parked across the street from the Moreno residence.

c. It was struck by the armored truck.

d. It was unoccupied at the time of the accident.

BOOK TWO

This is a test of your reading ability. In the following passages, words have been omitted. Each numbered set of dashed blank lines indicates where a word is left out; each dash represents one letter of the missing word. The correct word should not only make sense in the sentence but also have the number of letters indicated by the dashes.

Read through the whole passage, and then begin filling in the missing words. Fill in as many missing words as possible. If you aren't sure of the answer, take a guess.

Then mark your answers on the answer sheet as follows: Write the **first letter** of the word you have chosen in the square under the number of the word. Then blacken the circle of that letter of the alphabet under the square.

Only the blackened alphabet circles will be scored. The words you write on this page and the letters you write at the top of the column on the answer sheet **will not be scored.** Make sure that you blacken the appropriate circle in each column.

Some people say there is too little respect for the law. I say there is **1)** _ _ _ much respect for it. When people **2)** _ _ _ _ _ _ _ the law too much, they will **3)** _ _ _ _ _ _ it blindly. They will say, the majority has decided on this **4)** _ _ _, therefore I must heed it. They will not **5)** _ _ _ _ to consider whether or not the law is fair. If they do think the law is **6)** _ _ _ _ _, they think it is even more wrong to **7)** _ _ _ _ _ _ _ it. They **8)** _ _ _ _ _ _ _ that people must not break the law but must live with it until the majority has been persuaded to **9)** _ _ _ _ _ _ it. For example, many people in Birmingham, Alabama, knew that the laws that made black people **10)** _ _ _ _ up their seats on **11)** _ _ _ _ _ to white people were unjust. However, it was not **12)** _ _ _ _ _ Rosa Parks (an otherwise law-abiding **13)** _ _ _ _ _ _ _) refused to stand up and so **14)** _ _ _ _ _ _ the law that change came about. I am not saying that we should **15)** _ _ _ _ _ laws because they are inconvenient to **16)** _ _. I am saying that we must listen **17)** _ _ our consciences first. Only **18)** _ _ _ _ should we follow the law. If we know in our **19)** _ _ _ _ _ _ that the law is wrong, it is **20)** _ _ _ duty to break it.

(continued on page 17)

Americans like to believe that a juror's race **21**) _ _ _ _ _ absolutely no part in reaching a verdict. It **22**) _ _ becoming increasingly clear, however, that this is not always **23**) _ _ _ _. In fact, there seems to be a trend toward **24**) _ _ _ _ _ _ _ _ influenced verdicts, at least in certain urban areas with large **25**) _ _ _ _ _ _ _ _ populations. Some observers deplore this **26**) _ _ _ _ _. Others, however, argue that the trend is the latest manifestation of **27**) _ _ _ American tradition of jury nullification. Jurors do have the power, affirmed by the Supreme **28**) _ _ _ _ _ a hundred years ago, to set aside the law in favor of their own opinions **29**) _ _ _ _ they believe the law is wrong. Because the Constitution forbids trying a person twice for the **30**) _ _ _ _ crime, an acquittal cannot be overturned on the grounds that the jury ignored the **31**) _ _ _. American colonists used this principle before the Revolution **32**) _ _ acquit fellow **33**) _ _ _ _ _ _ _ _ of crimes against the Crown. Later, in the nineteenth **34**) _ _ _ _ _ _ _, antislavery jurors would acquit people who sheltered runaway **35**) _ _ _ _ _ _ even though doing so was a **36**) _ _ _ _ _. Some observers say that **37**) _ _ _ _ nullification is a legitimate weapon for black people to **38**) _ _ _ in a legal system **39**) _ _ _ _ they see (often with good **40**) _ _ _ _ _ _) as biased against them.

ANSWER KEY
BOOK ONE

PART ONE: CLARITY

1. **c.** The word *returned* is in the past tense, as are *finished* and *left* in the first part of the sentence, so this sentence is the only one that uses proper parallel structure.

2. **a.** The other choices contain sentence fragments.

3. **c.** *However* is the clearest and most logical transitional word.

4. **d.** The correct form of the verb is *sniffed.*

5. **c.** *To remove* and *lie* are the logical forms of these verbs.

6. **b.** Answers **a** and **d** are run-on sentences; **c** contains a sentence fragment.

7. **c.** There is no unnecessary shift in person; the other choices contain unnecessary shifts in person from *police officer* to *you, one,* and *we.*

8. **b.** No connecting word is needed to relate the first half of the sentence to the second. Connecting words in the other choices turn them into sentence fragments.

9. **b.** In **a, c,** and **d** the pronoun reference is ambiguous—who's in the hospital? Answer **c** also contains a misplaced modifier, *When in the hospital,* which seems to refer to *a phone call.*

10. **d.** The other answers contain unnecessary shifts in person from *I* to *one, you,* and *a person.*

11. **a.** The subject, *Lieutenant Jenny Crabtree,* and verb, *has written,* agree in number; in the other choices, subject and verb do not agree in number.

12. **b.** This is the only choice that does not contain a sentence fragment.

13. **d.** *However* is the clearest and most logical transitional word for these two ideas; the other choices contain less logical transitional words.

14. **a.** Answers **b** and **c** are sentence fragments. Answer **d** represents confused sentence structure as well as lack of agreement between subject and verb.

15. **d.** The correct verb form is *had drunk.*

PART TWO: VOCABULARY

16. b.
17. a.
18. d.
19. c.
20. c.
21. d.
22. b.
23. c.
24. a.
25. d.
26. a.
27. b.
28. b.
29. c.
30. d.

PART THREE: SPELLING

31. d.
32. a.
33. b.
34. a.
35. c.

36. a.

37. d.

38. b.

39. c.

40. d.

41. a.

42. c.

43. b.

44. a.

45. c.

PART FOUR: READING COMPREHENSION

46. c. This idea is stated in the second sentence and discussed throughout the passage.

47. b. Proof of guilt is the whole point of gathering evidence, but this is never referred to in the passage.

48. c. This is stated in the third sentence. Answer a is incorrect because, while rules of evidence protect the accused, that is not the reason the passage gives that an officer must know them.

49. a. The *pragmatic*, or *practical*, intent the author refers to in the third sentence is the purpose of shaping police procedure before arrest.

50. c. See paragraphs 3 and 4. The other answer choices are mentioned in the passage but are not the central argument.

51. b. See the last sentences of paragraph 1, which discusses the stalking victim's "worst fear."

52. d. All of the other choices are mentioned in the third paragraph. The victim's knowledge or lack of knowledge about anti-stalking laws is not discussed in the passage.

53. a. As discussed in the first paragraph, a restraining order is a civil remedy that is often not taken seriously by the stalker.

54. a. See the second paragraph. Answers b and c apply only to the Orange County woman; answer d cannot be shown to apply to either woman.

55. c. All three of the other choices are mentioned in the final paragraph.

56. c. While b and d are also true, they are not the main idea, which is supported by the whole passage and spelled out in the last sentence.

57. b. This is implied in the next-to-last sentence.

58. c. See the first sentence of the passage.

59. b. Miranda rights are read only when the suspect is taken into custody. The right to call a lawyer (c) and the right to a phone call (d) are included in the Miranda rights.

60. c. Officer Rayburn was on the scene first; the other officers arrived later, and the police operator was never on the scene.

61. a. The Woolf vehicle had stopped at the "T" intersection before turning on to Morton, so there must have been a stop sign on Farley. Burroughs was cited for failing to obey a stop sign on Morton.

62. b. Mr. Wilcox told Lieutenant Watts that the armored truck struck the car he was riding in, driven by Mr. Woolf, and that the Woolf vehicle subsequently hit Mrs. Moreno's car.

63. d. Officer Parisi examined skid marks, which show that the armored truck was braking.

64. a. The green sedan, with Mr. Woolf driving, had been driving down Farley before turning on to Morton at the "T" intersection.

65. d. Mrs. Moreno was in her house at the time of the accident.

BOOK TWO

1. too	**15.** break	**29.** when
2. respect	**16.** us	**30.** same
3. follow	**17.** to	**31.** law
4. law	**18.** then	**32.** to
5. stop	**19.** hearts	**33.** colonists
6. wrong	**20.** our	**34.** century
7. disobey	**21.** plays	**35.** slaves
8. believe	**22.** is	**36.** crime
9. change	**23.** true	**37.** jury
10. give	**24.** racially	**38.** use
11. buses	**25.** minority	**39.** that
12. until	**26.** trend	**40.** reason
13. citizen	**27.** the	
14. defied	**28.** Court	

SCORING

To pass the California POST test, you need a *score* of 70. But that 70 doesn't necessarily mean 70 questions right. The number of correct answers you need for a score of 70 changes each time the test is given. A good estimate of a passing score is 70%, or 74 questions right.

If you didn't do as well as you would like, analyze the reasons. Did you run out of time or feel rushed so that you made careless mistakes? Then you should work on pacing yourself through the exam. Did you do pretty well on some areas of the test and less well on others? Then you know where to concentrate further study. Did you have plenty of time but just not do well on any parts of the exam? Then you might need to spend a lot more time studying before you take the test. A refresher course in reading and writing skills at your local high school or community college might be in order.

What comes next? Here's what you should do based on your total number of right answers on this test.

WHAT'S NEXT	
If you scored:	**Your next step should be to:**
Below 70	Do some concentrated work in the areas you're weakest in. Use some of the additional resources listed in Chapters 7–10.
70–80	Review all of the instructional material in this book and perhaps get some additional help from a smart friend or teacher—just to be on the safe side.
Above 80	Relax. You're prepared. Review this book again before the exam if it will make you feel better.

C·H·A·P·T·E·R 12

THE PHYSICAL ABILITY TEST

CHAPTER SUMMARY

This chapter presents an overview of what to expect on the physical test you'll take on the way to becoming a state trooper. It also offers specific advice on how to get in shape for this often-demanding exam—and how to stay in shape.

Physical fitness testing, otherwise known as the physical ability or physical agility test, is a staple in the law enforcement selection process. In an attempt to measure your ability to successfully perform the duties of a law enforcement officer or to complete the training to perform those duties, an agency will in all probability require you to perform a test or series of tests that will physically challenge you. The timing as well as the make-up of the test are dictated to a certain extent by legislation that protects against potentially discriminatory practices. The goal of this chapter is to identify the types of tests you are likely to encounter and to provide you with some instruction—so that you can run and jump and push and pull your way through the selection test.

Tests to measure your physical ability to be a law enforcement officer generally take one of two forms: what's known as "job task simulation" and physical fitness. Physical fitness tests are widely used and favored for their validity and predictability. A battery of tests measure your physiological parameters, such as body composition, aerobic capacity, muscular strength and endurance, and flexibility. Physical fitness tests also hint at your medical status and, perhaps more important, they reveal your ability to perform the potentially hundreds of physical tasks required of a law enforcement officer.

Job task simulation tests, on the other hand, while they may tax your physiological fitness, are designed for the most part to illustrate your ability in a handful of job areas. Typically these tests also challenge your motor skills: balance, coordination, power, speed, reaction time, and agility.

Physical Fitness Tests

Physical fitness testing typically takes place in a group setting, most often in a gymnasium, field house, or athletic field—remember, these are "field tests." Attire for a day of testing is usually casual—sweats and sneakers—unless it occurs on the same day as other screening activities, such as a written exam. The time between events and the duration of the test vary according to the number of candidates and the number of test events.

Be prepared for the test. Bring water, nonperishable, easily digested "fuel foods" such as fruits and grains (bagels or bread), and a change of clothes in the event locker and shower facilities are available. At least one positive picture identification, black pens, and writing paper should also be in your bag.

Physical fitness test events typically include some *aerobic capacity test*, which measures your cardiorespiratory system's ability to take in and use oxygen to sustain activity. A field test, such as a one and one-half mile run or a 12-minute run, give an indication of your ability to participate in sustained activities such as walking a patrol, foot pursuits, and subject control and restraint. The most common standards here are "time to complete the distance" and "distance covered in the allotted time."

Flexibility, the ability to freely use the range of motion available at a given joint in your body, is fre-

quently tested because it impacts upon many movements and activities. Sitting for long periods at a dispatching center or behind the wheel of a patrol car or bending over to lift a handcuffed subject—all will affect or be affected by your flexibility. *Sit and reach tests* to evaluate low back and hamstring flexibility require you to sit with straight legs extended and to reach as far forward as possible. The performance standard for this commonly used test is to touch or to go beyond your toes.

Another staple of fitness tests are muscular strength and endurance measures. Muscular strength, the ability to generate maximum force, is indicative of your potential in a "use-of-force" encounter, subject control, or other emergency situation. *Bench press* and *leg press tests* to measure upper and lower body strength are commonly used and require you to lift a percentage of your present body weight. A maximum effort is required after a warm-up on the testing machine/apparatus.

Dynamic muscular endurance, on the other hand, is the ability to sustain effort over time. This very common element of fitness tests is related to sitting or standing for long periods of time as well as to the incidence of low back pain and disability. *Sit-up* and *push-up tests* are frequently timed events lasting one to two minutes that involve military push-ups and traditional or hands-across-the-chest sit-ups.

Finally, it is not uncommon to encounter a test that estimates the amount of fat compared to lean tissue or total body weight. *Body composition* is an indication of health risk status, and the results are usually expressed as a percent. Normal ranges for healthy young adults are 18-24% for females and 12-18% for males. A skinfold technique that measures the thickness of the skin and subcutaneous fat at sex-specific sites is the most common field test to estimate overall percentage of body fat.

Job Task Simulation Tests

Job task simulation tests use a small sample of actual or simulated job tasks to evaluate your ability to do the job of a law enforcement officer. This type of test is used because of its realistic relationship to the job and law enforcement training and because of its defensibility as a fair measure of a candidate's physical abilities.

Because courts of law have found it unreasonable to evaluate skills that require prior training, general job-related skills are tested at the applicant level. It's unlikely that you will be required to demonstrate competency with a firearm or handcuffs, for example. But climbing through a window, over barriers, and up stairs and use-of-force situations, such as a takedown or simulated application of handcuffs, are common tasks.

Simulation tests are often presented as obstacle courses, with the events performed one after another and linked by laps around the gymnasium or athletic field. Frequently, the requirement is to successfully complete the course or each event in a given amount of time. The test may be given on an individual or small group basis. Candidates performing a job task simulation test may be walked or talked through the first run or allowed to practice certain events prior to actual testing.

A job task simulation test is typically held during one of two periods, subject to labor and anti-discrimination legislation. Testing can legally occur at the very beginning of the process, alone or in combination with a written test, to establish an applicant's rank. Or it can take place after a written test but before a conditional offer of employment. In some cases, it may also occur following a conditional offer of employment. If this is the case you can reasonably expect a medical examination prior to participating in the test, which may also serve as an academy selection test. Due to the variability in the timing of the test, it is advisable to ask about physical standards as early in the selection process as possible.

IMPORTANT:
Regardless of the type of physical test you take, you need to be reasonably fit to successfully complete the test. Because the selection process, law enforcement training, and lifestyle of law enforcement officers are all stressful, it is essential to achieve fitness early and to maintain it for the duration of your law enforcement career.

Training Tips

In preparing for a physical fitness test, you must plan ahead, taking into account both the timing and the content of the test. The short-term objective, of course, is to pass the test. But your greater goal is to integrate fitness into your lifestyle so that you can withstand the rigors of the career you want in law enforcement.

The first order of business is to determine the type of fitness test you'll have to complete. What you have to accomplish on the test naturally will guide your training program. You can tailor your training to simulate the test and to train for the test events. Even if you're facing a job task test, you may want to include physical fitness test events, such as push-ups and sit-ups, in your training regimen. It's unsafe and inadequate to use skill events as your only training mode. If you're unfit it won't allow for a slow progression and if you are fit it may not represent enough of a challenge for you.

Following some basic training principles will help you create a safe and effective training program. Steady progress is the name of the game. Remember, you didn't get into or out of shape overnight, so you won't be able to change your condition overnight. To avoid injury while achieving overall fitness, balance in fitness training is essential. Work opposing muscle groups when doing strength or flexibility training and include aerobic conditioning as well as proper nutrition in your total fitness program.

To achieve continued growth in fitness you must overload the body's systems. The body makes progress by adapting to increasing demands. With adaptation, your systems are able to overcome the physical challenge, resulting in a higher level of fitness.

Finally, don't forget rest. It allows the body and the mind to recover from the challenges of training—and to prepare for another day.

12 Weeks to the Test Date

Your primary goal when faced with a short window of preparation is to meet a given standard, either physical fitness or job task simulation. Therefore, "specificity of training"—training for what you will actually be asked to do on the test—is the rule.

If you're training for a physical fitness test, then the performance standards are your training goals. You should make every attempt to use or to build up to the standards as the training intensity level. If you

---

STAYING "FITT"

FITT stands for Frequency, Intensity, Type, and Time. FITT simplifies your training by helping you plan what to do, when, how hard, and for how long. Because the four FITT "variables" are interrelated, you need to be careful in how you exercise. For example, intensity and time have an inverse relationship: as the intensity of your effort increases, the length of time you can maintain that effort decreases. A good rule of thumb when adjusting your workout variables to achieve optimum conditioning is to modify one at a time, increasing by 5-10%. Be sure to allow your body to adapt before adjusting up again.

The following presents some FITT guidelines to help you plan your training program.

Frequency
- 3-5 times a week

Intensity
- Aerobic training—60-85% of maximum effort
- Resistance training—8-12 repetitions
- Flexibility training—Just to slight tension

Type
- Aerobic—Bike, walk, jog, swim
- Resistance—Free weights, weight machines, calisthenics
- Flexibility—Static stretching

Time
- Aerobic—20-60 minutes
- Resistance—1-3 sets, 2-4 exercises/body part
- Flexibility—Hold stretched position 8-30 seconds

are unable to reach the standards right away, approximate them and increase the intensity 5% per week until you achieve them.

If you're training for a pre-academy test, try to determine what the academy's "PT" curriculum entails, use these as your modes of training, and test yourself with the standards every two to three weeks.

On the other hand, if the short-term goal is to meet a job task simulation test standard, particularly one that is used for pre-academy selection, you should determine the content of the PT curriculum and use it as the training model. At the same time, practice the skills required on the test once every two weeks in lieu of a training day.

Six or More Months to Go

The training program when there are six or more months to prepare is essentially similar to the one described above. However, the longer timeframe means that your goal can become making permanent, positive changes in your lifestyle rather than simply applying training principles to pass a test. Reasonable and gradual changes in your lifestyle will help to ensure that the behavioral and physical changes are permanent.

This extended timetable also reduces the likelihood of injury and allows for more diversity and balance in your training program and lifestyle. If you're preparing for a physical fitness test, you have the opportunity to set (and meet) performance goals that may be 25-50% greater than the standards themselves. On the other hand, if you have more than six months to prepare for a job task simulation test, you may want to avoid practicing any of the skills required for the first three months to avoid injury. Instead, consider incorporating sports activities into your conditioning routine; this will provide an enjoyable opportunity to train the necessary motor skills. After three months, you could begin practicing the physical test skills one day every two to four weeks.

A Sample Exercise Program

All of the information in this chapter about training principles and practices is put into action on the gym floor. A page taken from the academy physical fitness training book will help to get you fit and ready to excel in the physical test.

Physical training begins with a warm-up to increase your core body temperature and to prepare you for the more intense conditioning to follow. Brisk walking or jogging, in place or around a gymnasium, or jumping rope are good start-up options and should be conducted for three to five minutes. This is followed immediately by a period of active head-to-toe stretching to prevent injury.

Basic conditioning in the academy frequently is achieved with calisthenic exercises. Beginners can do sets of 10 on a "two count" and those of intermediate or advanced fitness can begin on a "four count" (1,2,3,1; 1,2,3,2; etc.). Running in formation typically follows 'cals' and is done at about a 9-10 minute per mile pace. Marine Corps cadences played on a Walkman may help to put you in the mood for academy runs! For those who are just beginning to prepare for the fitness test, 8-12 minutes of running is a safe start; those more fit may begin with 25 or more minutes. A three to five minute cooldown period to recover and some gentle, static stretching from the floor, focusing on the lower legs, will complete your workout and prepare you for the showers!

SAMPLE CALISTHENICS

Here are some recommended calisthenics to help get you in shape:

- Side straddle hop (jumping jacks)
- Half squats
- Heel raises
- Push-ups
- Stomach crunches

And for the more advanced:

- Diamond push-ups
- Bent leg raises

C·H·A·P·T·E·R 13

THE PERSONAL HISTORY STATEMENT

CHAPTER SUMMARY

Paperwork tells the tale—and you only get one shot at this document. This chapter explores the quirks, subtleties, and realities of the most critical phase of the application process. Ignore the advice here and chances are you'll be reading a letter of rejection!

The Personal History Statement is exactly that—a detailed personal statement of your life history. You may hear it called many things—the Application and the Applicant History Statement being the other common terms. No doubt you will come up with a few of your own by the time you finish this project. Although the paperwork may go by different names, the reason for jumping through these hoops is the same. The purpose of the statement is to provide law enforcement background investigators with the material for a panel, an individual, or a personnel department to make a sound decision about hiring you.

Not For The Faint of Heart

When you take your first look at the Personal History Statement, you might want to be sitting down. Or at least have a chair handy. This document can be a black hole for the unprepared. All of your precious time, energy, and resources will be sucked into the void if you aren't prepared to be asked for the tiniest details of your life. Although not all departments require the same level of detail, don't be surprised to find yourself madly hunting for the address of that kindergarten you once attended.

Some agencies aren't so demanding. They'll ask you to start out this tale of your life with your high school days and work forward. It's best to expect the worst, though. As one investigator told an applicant in Austin, Texas, "By the time I'm through going through the information in this document, I'll know whether or not you were breast fed as a child." He was.

This Size Fits All

No matter where you choose to apply, this chapter may be the helping hand you need to make your background investigation go as smoothly as possible. It will serve as a guide to help you present an accurate, HONEST summary of your past and present life. After all, the Personal History Statement—how you complete it, what you reveal and what you don't reveal—can determine whether or not you get the opportunity to convince an oral board you are worth hiring.

You may not make the connection between the oral interview board and the Personal History Statement at first. The connection is there and it's strong. What you reveal—and what you fail to reveal—in your Personal History Statement will come back around to help or haunt you at your oral board. Background investigators will rustle around in your life's basement using this document as a flashlight. They'll illuminate the good things and the bad things for all the oral board members to see and to use in their questioning. You're forewarned, however, and you are ready.

Different Methods—Same Results

One of the more frustrating aspects of searching for that perfect state police job is realizing that every state has

its own way of doing business. Yes, you may have applied yesterday to the New Jersey State Police, but today you may be filling out paperwork for the California Highway Patrol. Law enforcement agencies rarely have the same priorities, budgets, or staffing so the process, right down to the people they may want to hire, won't match up.

Be flexible. No matter how the application process is designed, no matter what order you handle each task given you, information you will need to supply each department remains the same. They all want to know about your past, present, and potential.

No Need To Wait

Even if you haven't decided which departments you will grace with your applications, you can start work now. Beginning with the day you were born, make a list of every address where you've lived up to the present. If you are 34 years old and normally change addresses twice a year you can pause a moment now to groan aloud. Make this list and keep plenty of copies. You'll only need to do this once instead of every time you apply to a different department if you are careful to keep copies of your efforts. Since your crystal ball works about like everyone else's, you can't be too sure what's in the future. The CIA, FBI, or other agency may lure you from your dream department one day and you'll wish you'd kept up the list.

Addresses aren't the only project you can work on ahead of time. Create a list of every part-time, full-time, some-time job you've had since your working life began. Once again, not every agency will use the same jump-off point to investigate your job history. Many forms ask you to list the jobs you've held during the past ten years, some during the past five years, and the others want your history from the moment you received your first check.

And There's Always...

Tickets. Here's yet another project to work on before applying to be a state police officer. Research your driving history. You'll be asked by some agencies to list every traffic ticket you've ever received in any state or country, whether on a military post or on civilian roadways. Some may ask you to list only the moving violations (these include speeding, running red lights, unsafe lane changes, etc.) while other agencies want to see moving violations and tickets for things like expired license plates, failure to wear seat belts, and most certainly expired automobile insurance.

One agency may ask for you to tell them about the tickets you've received in the past five years while others want to know your driving history from the moment your foot first touched an accelerator. Do your homework. And don't leave off tickets you think they won't find out about, because that kind of ticket doesn't exist. Tickets leave paper trails and paper trails are the easiest kinds to follow.

Dig These Up ASAP

Your pre-application preparations wouldn't be complete without a list of documents you'll need to have handy. This list does not include *every* form you may have to cough up, but it's almost a dead certainty you will need:

- Birth Certificate
- Social Security Card
- DD 214 (if you are a veteran)
- Naturalization papers (if applicable)
- High School Diploma or G.E.D. Certificate
- High School Transcripts
- College Transcripts
- Current Driver's License(s)
- Current Copies of Driving Records
- Current Consumer Credit Reports

If you don't have certified copies of these above-listed documents, start calling or writing the proper authorities *now* to find out what you need to do to get them. If you've sucked your social security card up in the vacuum cleaner and haven't seen it since, run down to the social security office in your community and arrange for a new one. Legal documents often take anywhere from six to eight weeks for delivery, but you probably won't be able to wait that long if you have already received and started on your Personal History Statement. Most agencies have a deadline for filling out and returning Personal History Statements so you may have to tap dance a bit.

If time runs out and you realize you won't be able to turn the Personal History Statement in with all the required documents, *ask* the powers-that-be what you should do. Many agencies will tell you to attach a memo to your application outlining your problem and what you have done about it. For example, you've ordered a copy of your birth certificate but either the postal service is using it for scratch paper or your request is mired in the bureaucratic process. Attach a letter of explanation to your application detailing when you requested a copy of your birth certificate, where you asked for the copy to be sent, and when you expect to receive the document. If you have it, attach all copies of correspondence you sent out requesting a copy of your certificate. That'll show that you are making all the right moves.

Check First

You have a little homework to do before rounding up all of these documents. Check with as many agencies as you can to find out what rules they have for how certain documents are submitted—like college transcripts, for instance. Agency officials may require you to have the school send the documentation directly to their recruiting office instead of to you at home via regular mail. The same goes for credit reports or copies of driving records. It's best to call the recruiting department, explain to them that you are trying to round up all of your documentation, and ask them how they accept these documents so you'll know what to do.

Other questions you need to ask are:

- Do you need photocopies or original documents?
- Will you return my original if I send it?
- How recent does the credit history have to be?
- What's the most recent copy you will accept of my college transcript?

The answers to these questions can save you lots of money on antacids and postage. You'd be surprised at the number of ways each agency can come up with for you to chase paper.

READY FOR ACTION

So, you're as prepared as you can be. You've made your decision on where you are applying and let's even assume you are at the point in the application process where you've received the Personal History Statement. *Before* you set pen to paper, make a copy of this form. Do not write on it, breathe on it, or dare to set it down on the coffee table without having a copy made FIRST. After you have a copy, then put away the original for now. (You'll be using the photocopy as a working draft and a place to make mistakes.) Eventually you will transfer all the information you have on your practice copy onto the original. You may be spending lots of time on this project and using more than a few dimes in the copy machine before this is all over, but it'll be time and money well spent. Especially if the *unthinkable* happens. And the unthinkable usually goes like this:

Your phone rings. It's your recruiter. "Gee, Fred, this is Trooper Jones in recruiting and I have a little bad news. We can't seem to put a finger on that application you sent. Isn't that the darndest thing? Could you make us a copy from the one you have at home and send it out right away?"

Don't think it doesn't happen. Be sure to make copies of the application and accompanying documentation you submit and keep them in a safe place. And hold on to these copies! You need to review this document before the oral board gets ahold of you, not to mention the possibility that you may need this information to complete other applications for other adventures years down the road.

Personal History Statements may vary from agency to agency, but the questions most applicants ask about these tedious documents have not changed over the years. The following are a few questions and comments made by actual applicants as they went through application processes across the U.S. The responses made to these questions and comments will allow you to learn from someone else's mistakes, thereby giving you an advantage over the competition—and having an advantage in this highly competitive field can never hurt!

"What do you mean you don't accept resumes? It cost me $60 to get this one done!"

A formal resume like one you may prepare for a civilian job is usually not much good to a law enforcement agency. Although criminal justice instructors in many colleges suggest to their students to have a resume made, it's always best to call and ask a recruiter whether or not to bother. Why go to the expense if the agency is going to throw away the resume upon receipt? Most agencies will rely upon their Personal History Statements to get the details of your life, education, and experience, so save yourself time and dimes when you can.

Those dimes will come in handy at the copy machine when you make backup copies of your Personal History Statement!

"I didn't realize the Personal History Statement would take so long to complete and the deadline for turning it in caught me by surprise. I got in a hurry and left some things blank."

The letter this applicant received in the mail disqualifying her from further consideration probably caught her by surprise as well. As you know from reading this chapter so far, a Personal History Statement requires planning, efficiency, and attention to detail. Most agencies demand accuracy, thoroughness, and timeliness. There are entirely too many applicants to choose from who have taken the time necessary to properly fill out an application for a busy background investigator to bother with an applicant who has left half of the form blank and isn't quite sure what should go in the other half. In fact, many agencies will tell you up front in their application instructions that failing to respond to questions or failure to provide requested information can result in disqualification.

"I read *most* of the instructions. I didn't see the part that said I had to print."

Read *all* of the instructions. Every sentence. Every word. And please do so before you begin filling out your practice copy of the Personal History Statement. In fact, you need to read the entire document from the first page to the last page before you tackle this project. Have a note pad next to you and as you read make notes of everything you do not understand. You'll be making a phone call to your recruiter AFTER reading the entire document to ask questions. It's important to read the whole document because the questions on your pad may be answered as you read along. It's a bit embar-

rassing to call with a question that the recruiter answers by saying "Well, as you would have found out by reading the next sentence, you should...."

"No one is going to follow up on all this stuff anyway. It'd take way too long and it's way too involved."

A good background investigator lives for the opportunity to follow up on the details of your life. That's their job. When all is said and done, they must sign their name at the bottom of the report documenting their investigation. It's not wise to assume someone will put their career at risk by doing a sloppy job on your background investigation. A thorough investigator will take as much time as it takes to do a good job. The good news is that you can earn brownie points by making that investigator's job as simple as possible. Give them as much information as you possibly can and make that information RIGHT. When you write down a phone number, make sure it's correct. For example, if you used to work at Jumpin' Jacks Coffee Parlor four years ago and you still remember the phone number, CALL that number to make sure it's correct before you write it down. Nothing is more irritating to a busy investigator than dialing wrong number after wrong number. If that's the only number you have and you discover it's no longer in service, make a note of this so the investigator doesn't assume you are being sloppy. Phone numbers get changed and businesses go under every day.

When you turn in a Personal History Statement you are building on the reputation you began forming from the moment you first made contact with recruiting staff. An application that is turned in on time, is filled out neatly and meticulously, and that has *correct*, detailed information that is easily verified says a lot about the person who filled it out. Not only will an investigator have warm fuzzy thoughts for anyone who makes his/her job easier, they will come to the conclusion that you will probably carry over these same traits into your work as a state police officer.

The investigator, the oral board, and the staff psychologist all will be looking at HOW you filled out the application as well as what information is contained in the application. Investigators will build a case for hiring you (or *not* hiring you) based on facts, impressions, and sometimes even intuition. With this in mind, *every detail is worth a second look* before you call your Personal History Statement complete. Ask yourself:

- Is my handwriting as neat as it can be?
- Did I leave off answers or skip blanks?
- Do my sentences make sense?
- Is my spelling accurate?
- Are my dates and times consistent?

"I figured you could find out that information easier than I could. That's why I didn't look up that information. After all, you're the investigator."

And this applicant is probably *still* looking for a job. The Personal History Statement is a prime opportunity for you to showcase your superb organizational skills, knack for detail, and professionalism. Do as much of the work as you can for the background investigator. Make your extra credit points where you can. For example, let's say you worked for Grace's High Heels and Muffler Emporium. The business went under after a few months, much to everyone's surprise, and you moved on to other employment. You're not sure what happened to Grace, your immediate supervisor and owner of the business, but you do know a friend of hers. Contact that friend, find out Grace's address and phone number, and give this information to your investigator. Yes, the investigator probably would find her on his/her own, but you went the extra mile, you showed the initiative, and you are going to get the brownie points.

It's not uncommon for state public safety agencies to get thousands of applications per year. Most of the applicants have the same credentials to offer as you do. Do all you can do to stand out from the crowd. Nothing gets noticed faster than efficiency, professionalism, and accuracy. Well, that's not quite right. Inaccuracies, sloppiness, and laziness usually win first notice.

"I know I got disqualified, but it's only because I misunderstood the question. I didn't want to ask about it because I didn't want to look dumb."

If you do not understand a question—ASK someone. By not making sure you know how to properly answer a question you run the risk of answering it incorrectly, incompletely, or not at all. Any one of these mistakes can lead to your disqualification if an investigator thinks you are not telling the truth, or that you are unwilling to provide the information requested. Don't take chances when a simple question will clear up the problem.

"You know, I didn't have any idea what that question meant so I just guessed."

Never guess. Never assume. This advice can never be repeated too often—if you don't know, find out. ASK QUESTIONS. Answering them is part of the job for recruiters or background investigators.

"I lied because I thought if I told the truth, I'd look bad."

Never lie about *anything*. As far as law enforcement professionals are concerned, there is no such thing as a harmless lie. Supervisors don't want people working for them who cannot tell the truth, other troopers don't want to work with partners whom they can't trust, and citizens expect *criminals* to lie, not state police officers. Your credibility must be beyond reproach.

Let's look at an example. One applicant told his recruiter that the reason he didn't admit to getting a ticket for failing to have his car registered was because he thought the agency would think he wasn't organized and couldn't take care of business. Which would you prefer for a potential employer to know about you—that you lie instead of admitting to mistakes, or that you make mistakes and admit to them readily? The fact is, telling the truth is crucial if you want to be a state police officer.

"I listed John Doe as a personal reference because he's the mayor and I worked on his campaign. Why did my investigator call and make me give another reference?"

Choose your personal references carefully. Background investigators do not want to talk to people because they have impressive credentials. They want to talk to them so they can get a feel for how you are as a person. Investigators will know within minutes whether or not a reference knows you well. Personal references are important enough to warrant their own in-depth discussion later in this chapter, so read on.

HOW TO READ AND ANSWER QUESTIONS

Reading questions and instructions carefully is critical to successfully completing the Personal History Statement. Certain words should leap off the page at you. These are the words you should key in on:

- All
- Every
- Any
- Each

If you see these words in a question, you are being asked to include all the information you know. For example,

you may see the following set of instructions in your Personal History Statement:

List **any** and **all** pending criminal charges against you.

This doesn't mean list only the charges facing you in Arizona, but not the ones from that incident in Nevada last week. This agency wants to know about every single criminal charge that may be pending against you no matter what city, county, parish, village, country, or planet may be handling the case(s). Do not try to tap dance your way around instructions like these for any reason. If your fear is that the information you list might make you look bad, you may have some explaining to do. And you may have perfectly good explanations for your past and your present. If you lie or try to make yourself look good, chances are you'll be disqualified in short order and no one will get the opportunity to consider those explanations.

Another question you may see is:

Have you **ever** been arrested or taken into police custody for **any** reason?

The key words are **ever** and **any**. This agency means at any time in your life, beginning at your moment of birth, up to and including the split second that just went by. If you don't know what is meant by the term "arrested," then call your recruiter or investigator and ASK. Do not play the well-no-one-put-handcuffs-on-me-so-I-wasn't-really-under-arrest game. When in doubt, list any situation you think has a ghost of a chance of falling into the category you are working on. The best advice, though, is ASK IF YOU DON'T KNOW!

Here's a request for information that includes several eye-catching words.

List **all** traffic citations you received in the past five (5) years, in this or **any** other state (moving and non-moving) **excluding** parking tickets.

In this example, the agency leaves little doubt that what you should do here is make a complete list of every kind of violation you've been issued a citation for, no matter where you got it and no matter what the traffic violation was for within the past five years. They even let you know the one kind of citation they don't need to know about—parking tickets. If you aren't sure what a moving violation is or what a non-moving violation is, call the department and have them explain. Keep in mind that when the officer issued you a citation on a single piece of paper, you may have been cited for more than one violation. Most citations have blanks for at least three violations, sometimes more. For example, last year you were pulled over for speeding. The officer discovered you had no insurance and your car license plates were expired. She told you she was writing you three tickets for these violations, but handed you only one piece of paper. Did you get one citation or three? You got three.

Once again, ASK if you don't know. No one will make fun of you if you are unfamiliar with terminology such as "moving violation."

PERSONAL REFERENCES

Your personal references are the people who will be able to give the background investigator the best picture of you as a whole person. Some Personal History Statements ask you to list at least five people as references and some only ask for three. You also may be given a specific time limit for how long you may have known these people before listing them. Your instructions may direct you to list only those individuals whom you've known for a minimum of two years, for exam-

ple. Pay close attention to the instructions for this section, if there are any. Selecting the people for this area is not something you should take lightly for many reasons.

Earlier, you read that by making the investigator's job easier you make your investigation run smoother, you get brownie points, and your background is finished quickly. The Personal References Section is one area where you really want to make it easy. You'll want the investigator to talk to people who know you well—who can comment on your hobbies, interests, personality, and ability to interact with others. Try to choose friends who will be honest, open, and sincere. When an investigator calls a reference and figures out quickly that the person he/she is talking to barely has an idea of who you are, the red flags will come shooting up. Investigators are suspicious people by nature. Most law enforcement professionals are. The investigator will wonder why you listed someone who doesn't know you well. Are you trying to throw them off the track? Are you afraid someone who knows you too well will let out information you don't want known? This is how an investigator will look at the situation. And, at the very least, you'll get a phone call requesting another reference because the one you listed was unsatisfactory.

Most investigators expect for you to tell the personal references that you listed them and that they will be getting a phone call or a personal visit from the investigating agency. Get the RIGHT phone numbers, find out from your references what times they are most accessible, and ESPECIALLY find out if they have any objections to being contacted. You don't need a reluctant personal reference. They often do more harm than good.

Tell your references how important it is for them to be open and honest with the investigator. Let them know that if they do not understand a question, they should feel free to tell the investigator they don't understand. It's also wise to let them know that there are no right or wrong answers to most of these questions. Investigators do not want to have a conversation with someone who is terrified about saying the "wrong thing." And that's what your personal references should expect to have with an investigator—a conversation, not an interrogation. Your goal here is to let the investigator see you as a person through the eyes of those who know you best.

Looks Aren't Everything—Or Are They?

You've filled out the practice copy you made of the Personal History Statement, made all your mistakes on that copy, answered all the questions, and filled in all the appropriate blanks. Now you're ready to make the final copy.

Part of the impression you will make on those who have the hiring and firing decisions will come from how your application looks. Is your handwriting so sloppy that investigators pass your work around to see who can read it? Did you follow the instructions directing you to PRINT? Were you too lazy to attach an additional sheet of paper instead of writing up and down the sides of the page? Did you SPELL words correctly? Do your sentences make sense to the reader? (A good tip here is to read your answers out loud to yourself. If it doesn't make sense to your ear, then you need to work on what you wrote.)

Every contact you make with the hiring agency makes an impression. The written impression you make when you turn in your Personal History Statement is one that can follow you through the entire process and into the academy. In fact, it can have a bear-ing on whether or not you even make it into the academy because most departments have a method of scoring you on the document's appearance.

Here are some items you might find useful as you work on your application:

- a dictionary
- a grammar handbook
- a good pen (or pencil—whatever the directions tell you to use)
- a screaming case of paranoia

The paranoia will ensure that you check your work, check it again, and have someone you trust check it yet again *before* you make your final copy.

You now have the information you need to make the Personal History Statement a manageable task. This is not a document to take lightly, especially when you are now aware of the power this document has over your potential career as a state police officer. Remember, it's important that you:

- follow instructions and directions
- be honest and open about your past and present
- provide *accurate* information
- choose excellent personal references
- turn in presentable, error-free documentation
- turn in documents on time

A recruiting department can ask for nothing better than an applicant who takes this kind of care and interest in the application process. And you will get all the credit!

C·H·A·P·T·E·R 14

THE ORAL INTERVIEW

CHAPTER SUMMARY

This is the next best thing to having someone do your oral interview for you. The oral interview process is demystified in these pages with a down-to-earth look at the ordeal. Read on for tips, suggestions, and don't-do's.

Welcome to the board. Those are the words you want to hear. That means you've survived most of the process and are one step closer to your dream. State trooper. In Florida, applicants who hear that opening phrase will be stepping into a room with an oral board comprised of three members. This panel of higher-ranking professionals will take at least 20 minutes of your life to see if you have the strong communication skills necessary for such a demanding career. In Texas, trooper applicants will speak before a board of five interviewers ranging in rank from field trooper to lieutenant. You'll have 45 minutes to knock their socks off.

The oral interview board, no matter what form it takes, is unlike any oral job interview you will ever experience. The questions are pointed, personal, and uncompromising. Vague, plastic responses will usually goad a panel of veteran state police officers into rougher questioning techniques until they get the honest response called for by the circumstances. The information you are about to receive will show you how to prepare for the oral board from the moment you decide to apply to an agency until the moment the head of the board thanks you for your participation.

HIRE ME, PLEASE!

If you're like most people you've had some experience asking someone for a job. So, it's not unrealistic to expect that the trooper oral interview board will be similar to a civilian oral interview—is it? Yes and no. There are a few similarities. Both prospective civilian and law enforcement employers are looking for the most qualified person for the job—reliable, honest men and women who will work hard and be there when they are needed.

"Hire" Expectations

Civilian employers expect applicants to show up on time for their interview, dressed professionally, and showing off their best manners, as do state police employers. When you step into a trooper's oral interview board, however, you will realize that the people who are interviewing you have more than a surface interest in you and your past experiences. And the board will have more than a two-page resume in their hands when the interview begins.

Exactly who is going to be using the details of your personal and professional life to interview you? More than likely it will be a panel of two, three, four—maybe more—individuals with one purpose in mind: to get to know you well. The board members will most likely be supervisory-level troopers who have several years' experience on the force. Some departments use civilian personnel specialists to sit on their boards, but most interview boards will be made up of experienced troopers.

These board members will be using information you have provided on your application and information investigators discover during your background investigation. Investigators will provide board members with a detailed report on your past and present life history. Yes, you'll be asked questions when board members already know the answer and when they don't know the answer. You'll be asked to explain why you've made the decisions you've made in your life—both personal and professional. You'll also be asked questions that

don't have right or wrong answers. In short, you can expect an intense grilling from men and women who don't have the time or patience for applicants who walk into their interview unprepared.

Tell What You Know, Know What You Tell

Before you reach the oral interview board stage of the application process you will have had to fill out a detailed personal history statement often referred to as the Applicant History Statement, the Personal History Statement, or simply the application. Terminology differs from agency to agency. Unless you are skipping around in this book, you've probably read about it by now. Call it what you want—just don't underestimate its role in the oral interview.

The Personal History Statement guides the oral board through your past and present life. You must be willing to open your life up to the board by giving them an informative, ACCURATE tour of where you've been in your life and who you are.

Since the Personal History Statement is what background investigators use to conduct investigations and what a final report to the board is built on, then it follows that you should make that document your life when you are filling it out. Members of the oral board generally are given a copy of your Personal History Statement and then a copy of the investigators' final report on you. While you are answering questions for the board, most board members will be shuffling through the pages of your life—checking what you say against what they see on paper. Naturally, you'll want to remember what information you gave them. Instead of tossing and turning the night before your interview, your time will be well spent reading and rereading your Personal History Statement so that you know what they know about you.

How much effort you put into the Personal History Statement will have a direct impact on how difficult your oral interview will be. If board members have an accurate, detailed picture of you as a whole person from the information you have supplied, your time under the microscope will be less than the applicant who turned in a vague, mistake-laden account of his/her past and present life. If the thought of the oral interview board makes your palms sweat, then pay close attention to the chapter on how to handle the Personal History Statement. You'll feel better afterward.

There's Plenty of Time, Right?

Preparation for the oral interview board begins when you make the decision to apply. From the moment you first make contact with a recruiter, everything you say and do will be potential fuel for the oral interview board. Even walking through the doors of the recruiting office to pick up an application, you have the opportunity to make a lasting impression. You are dealing with professionals who are trained to notice and *remember* people and details.

If you show up to pick up an application wearing your favorite cutoff blue jeans and trashed out, beer-stained T-shirt from those college party days, you may be in for a shock several months later when a board member asks you why you chose to make that particular fashion statement. Dress neatly and as professionally as possible each and *every* time you make contact with the department where you want to work.

Same goes for telephone contacts—if you call a department to request an application you will make an impression on the person who answers the phone. If all you want is an information packet and/or application and you do not have any specific questions to ask, do NOT take this opportunity to tell the recruiter your entire life story from the moment of conception.

Not only are you probably the 100th person to request an application that day, the recruiter has no way, or reason, to remember the details of your life at this stage of the process. Remember, though, you have to give out your name and address to this person who will be responsible for mailing your application, so the potential for connecting your name to the impression you make on the phone is high.

As silly as it may make you feel, it's a good idea to practice what you say *before* you dial the phone. In fact, it's not a bad idea to write down what you'd like to say before you call. This will give you control over the impression you make and eliminate the possibility of the first words out of your mouth being: "uh... hi... I... uh... wanna... uh... Can you mail me a... uh... one of those... uh... I wanna be a trooper but I need a... application! Yeah, that's it!"

Do the same for any questions you may have. Make a list and as you ask each question, listen carefully to the response without interruption. Above all, never ask a question that is designed to show off how much you know. The chances of you knowing more about law enforcement than the person who is already working in the field is slim. Your opportunity to impress the agency will come later in the appropriate setting—the oral interview board.

Self-Awareness—Don't Show Up Without It!

You wouldn't want to show up for a car race on a tricycle, any more than you would want to try putting out a fire with gasoline. Using this same logic, it's safe to say you'd never want to sit down in front of a panel of professionals who have the power to offer you a career dealing with people without a good measure of self-awareness.

Self-awareness is knowing yourself—being aware of what you do and why you do it. Many of the questions you'll hear from the board are designed to reveal how well you know yourself and how honest you can be about your talents and your shortcomings.

Big Tip!

Do NOT pay any attention to consultants or books suggesting that you downplay, or do not admit to, weaknesses. If you can remember only one piece of advice from this chapter, please let it be this! If an oral board member asks you to list the weaknesses you believe you have and you can't think of any, they will be more than happy to bring up a few instances in your life to illustrate the weaknesses you aren't able to identify.

You should be able to list your weaknesses with the same unhesitating manner with which you list your strengths. And you should be able to tell the board what you are doing to correct or compensate for your weaknesses. If you truly aren't aware of your failings, ask trusted friends and relatives for their input. Write down what you think your weaknesses are and then compare your list with what your friends and family have said. Don't forget to ask them about your strengths as well. Some applicants find talking about strengths as difficult as talking about weaknesses. You must be able to do both.

Don't You Remember? YOU Put It On Your Application!

Part of being self-aware is knowing what others know about you. Hardly any of the questions during your oral board interview should come as a surprise to you if you have taken the copy of your application that you made *before* turning it in and studied it.

Before showing up for the board you must take the time to go back over your application and carefully think about each piece of information in this document. The questions put to you by the board are generated mostly from the information you write in the Personal History Statement. As you review your copy of the Statement, think about the questions such information could generate.

For example, if one of the questions on the application directed you to list any instances where you've been fired from a job, think about how you would answer the question, "Mr. Smith, can you tell the board why you got fired from Tread Lightly Tire Shop in 1993?" Although you may have told the investigator why you were fired during an earlier conversation, the board will want to hear it for themselves.

HELP YOURSELF!
Tame Public Speaking Fears

Being interviewed by a group of people is a lot like having one of those dreams where you show up to work in nothing but a pair of socks. You experience anxiety, sweaty palms, and a burning desire to be some place else. Public speaking classes will go a long way toward easing your fear of talking to groups.

Strongly consider taking a speech class at a nearby community college or through an adult education course. At the very least, have a friend ask you questions about yourself and have them take notes about any annoying mannerisms you may exhibit while speaking. Then practice your speaking and learn to control those mannerisms.

Practice is one of the keys to success on an oral board. If you've ever truly practiced something—batting a ball, for instance—you know that once you have the motion down you can rely on your muscles to "remember" what to do when it comes time to play the game. The same rationale holds true for practicing oral board answers.

One effective technique is to mentally place yourself in a situation and visualize how you want to act or respond when the pressure is on. Some troopers call this mental exercise "What if..." and they use this technique to formulate a plan of action for those times when split-second decisions rule the moment. Visualizing a successful performance ahead of time can help trigger that response once you're in the actual situation. This technique will work for you if you practice, practice, practice.

Right On Time? Tsk, Tsk!

Show the board how much you want this job. They'll check to see when you arrived for your board. An early arrival means you planned ahead for emergencies (flat tires, wrong turns, etc.), that you arrived in enough time to prepare yourself mentally for what you are about to do, and that you place a value on other people's time as well as your own.

Packaging Sells Product

You may feel like you don't have much control over what happens to you in an oral interview setting, but this is one area where you have total control. The initial impression you make on board members is up to you and this is the perfect opportunity to score points without ever opening your mouth. The way you dress sends a signal to the people who are watching you walk into the room.

Blue jeans and a "nice shirt" tells the panel you wouldn't mind having the job if someone wouldn't mind giving it to you. Business suits (for men and women) tell them you *want* this job, you take this interview seriously, and there's nothing casual about the way you are approaching it.

If you don't own businesswear, borrow it. Rent it. Buy it. Wear it! Chances are you've already invested time and money into the education necessary to get most criminal justice jobs. This is not the time to balk at spending money on appropriate clothing. Just go get the suit any way you can.

Make Mama Proud

After you've earned bonus points with your professional appearance, it's time to earn more with your manners. Most law enforcement agencies are paramilitary organizations—your first clue should be the uniforms and the rank structure. In the military it's customary to address higher-ranking men and women with courtesy.

"Yes, ma'am" or "yes, sir" or "no, ma'am" or "no, sir" is expected from military personnel. If you have military experience you will be ahead in this area.

If you are not accustomed to using these terms of courtesy, practice them! Make a conscious effort to use them. It's rarely considered rude to simply respond "yes" or "no" to a question, but you'll *always* be on shaky ground if "yeah" or "uh huh" are your customary responses.

Location is important. If you've flown from New York to Texas to apply for a job, you definitely do not want to say "yeah" or "what?" in your oral board. People in the South raise their children to say "yes, ma'am" and "no, sir" and hearing "huh?" or "yeah" is at best an irritant to southern ears. This may not be an issue in other parts of the nation, although it'd be a safe bet to assume many board members have either been in the military at some point in their lives or like the paramilitary structure of law enforcement. You won't go wrong with "yes, sir" instead of "yeah" or "Could you repeat the question?" instead of "what?"

No doubt you realize that an oral board sees many, many applicants when a department is in a hiring phase. Most oral boards typically schedule five or six applicants in one day for interviews. Some agencies schedule boards for one day during the week and some departments have oral boards set for every day of the week. The point here is that you are talking to people who are more than likely quite tired of listening. That means the "little things" take on an extra importance.

YES IT ALL MATTERS

What you've read so far may seem inconsequential. This is far from the truth. You walk a fine line when you appear before an oral board. They want you to appear self-confident and poised, but not cocky or arrogant. You're expected to be nervous, but not so nervous that you can't communicate beyond an occasional grunt or nod. You're expected to be polite, but you're not expected to fawn all over the board. Above all, you are expected to be yourself and not who you *imagine* the board might want. Which brings up another point— what exactly *is* the board looking for in an applicant?

People Talent—Gotta Have It

The men and women patrolling the highways today are expected to be highly responsive to the public they protect. Agency officials are looking for applicants who have excellent verbal skills and a strong desire to "be there" for the public. To give you an idea how most agencies feel about their mission, consider the motto for the Department of Public Safety troopers in Texas: "Service, Courtesy, and Protection." So, no, it's not a secret that the successful applicant will need superior people-handling skills. But what about skills that may be less obvious?

Oral interview boards are faced with the formidable task of hiring individuals who have the skills and talents equal to the demands of modern law enforcement. The men and women most highly sought after by agencies are those who are not only good with people, but with modern technology as well. When you open the door to your patrol car, the first thing to catch your eye might not necessarily be the radio and siren box. It may well be a computer. Computers are here to stay — in the office and on the road. If you think a keyboard is a chunk of wood you hang patrol car keys on, you are in for a surprise. You can bet your competition is in class hunched over a keyboard at this moment because they know oral boards love to hear "Why, certainly" to the question, "Have you ever used a computer?" If you haven't already, now's the time to brush up on your typing skills and sign up for a computer class.

Then there's the liability issue. Lawsuits and threats of lawsuits have law enforcement agencies scurrying to find applicants who have specific qualities and skills that will keep them out of the headlines and civil courtrooms.

Show Your Stuff

Yes, law enforcement agencies want it all. There's *always* room for men and women who can leap tall buildings and do the speeding train thing, but even if your cape isn't red, you can still compete if you can convince the board you have the following qualities:

- Maturity
- Common sense
- Good judgment
- Compassion
- Integrity
- Honesty
- Reliability
- The ability to work without constant supervision

These qualities aren't ranked in order of importance because it would be hard to say which should come first. They are all of importance in the eyes of the board and your task in the oral interview setting is to convince them you have these qualities. Since you are in an obvious question-and-answer setting, you'll do your convincing through how and what you say when you respond to questions.

YOUTH AND INEXPERIENCE— PLUS OR MINUS?

The question here is will an oral board think you have enough life experience for them to be willing to take a chance on hiring you. Local, state, and federal law enforcement agencies have never been as liability conscious as they are today. Incidents like the Rodney King trial and subsequent Los Angeles riots, not to mention the O. J. Simpson trial, have heightened the awareness of legal departments around the country.

This concern ripples straight through an agency and eventually arrives to haunt recruiters, background investigators, oral boards, and everyone who has anything to do with deciding who gets a badge. The first question you hear when trouble hits an agency is, "How did that person get a job here anyway?" As a result, applicants are scrutinized even more closely than ever before and agencies are clearly leaning toward individuals who have proven track records in employment, schooling, volunteer work, and community involvement.

Youth and inexperience are not going to disqualify you from the process. You should be aware that if you are 21 years old and have never held a job, have never been responsible for your own care, feeding, and life in general, you will have a more difficult time getting hired as a trooper than someone who is older, has job references to check, and who is able to demonstrate a history of reliability and responsibility.

Maturity is a huge concern with state agencies. They can no longer afford to hire men and women who are unable to take responsibility for their actions or the actions, in some cases, of those around them. Although maturity cannot be measured in the number of years an individual has been alive, departments will want to see as much proof as possible that you have enough maturity and potential to risk hiring you.

Get Out in the World

Make it as easy as possible for the oral board to see how well you handle responsibility. Sign up for volunteer work *now* if you don't have any experience dealing with people. If you are still living at home with parents, be able to demonstrate the ways in which you are responsible around the home. If you are on your own, but living with roommates, talking to the board about this experience and how you handle conflicts arising from living with strangers or friends will help your case.

You may want to work extra hard on your communication skills before going to the board. The more articulate you are the better you will be able to sell yourself and your potential to the board if you are young. Your need to open up and let the board see you as a worthy investment will be greater than an older applicant who has plenty of personal and business history to pour over.

Older and Wiser Pays Off

Being older certainly is not a hindrance in law enforcement. Oral boards are receptive to men and women who have life experience that can be examined, picked apart, and verified. Maturity, as has been mentioned before, is not necessarily linked with how old you are. Older applicants can be either blessed or cursed by the trail they've left in life. Many applicants have gone down in flames because they were unable to explain incidents in their past and present that point to their immaturity and inability to handle responsibility.

Applicants of any age who have listed numerous jobs and have turned in Personal History Statements too thick to run through a stapling machine should be extra-vigilant about doing homework before the oral board stage. If you fall into this category, you should carefully pour over the copy of the application your background investigator used to do your background check. Be fully aware of the problem areas and know what you will most likely be asked to explain. And decide now what you are going to say. Prepare, prepare, prepare.

Don't Leave The Meter Running

The longer your history, the longer you can expect to sit before an oral board. If a board is not required to adhere strictly to time limits, you may be required to endure a longer session than other applicants simply because there's more material to cover. The more you know about yourself and the more open you are about your life the smoother your interview will run. This advice holds true for *all* applicants.

THE NITTY-GRITTY

Questions. What kind of questions are they going to ask? Isn't that what everyone is really worried about when they are sitting in the chair labeled "NEXT" outside of the interview room? You will hear all kinds of questions—personal questions about your family life, questions about your likes and dislikes, questions about your temperament, your friends, and even a few designed to make you laugh so you'll get a little color back into your face. Don't look for many questions that can be answered with simply "yes" or "no" because you won't get that lucky. Let's look at the types of questions you are likely to hear.

Open-Ended Questions

The open-ended question is the one you are most likely to hear. An example of an open-ended question is:

Board Member: "Mr. Jones, can you tell the board about your Friday night bowling league?"

Board members like these questions because it gives them an opportunity to see how articulate you can be and it gives them a little insight into how you think. This is also a way for them to ease into more specific questions. Example:

Board Member: "Mr. Jones, can you tell the board about your Friday night bowling league?"
Jones: "Yes ma'am. I've been bowling in this league for about two years. We meet every Friday night around 6 p.m. and bowl until about 8:30 p.m. I like it because it gives me some-

thing to do with friends I may not get to see otherwise because everyone is so busy. This also gives me time to spend with my wife. We're in first place right now and I like it that way."
Board Member: "Oh, congratulations. You must be a pretty competitive bowler."
Jones: "Yes ma'am, I am. I like to win and I take the game pretty seriously."
Board Member: "How do you react when your team loses, Mr. Jones?"

That one question generates enough information for the board to draw a lot of conclusions about Mr. Jones. They can see that he likes to interact with his friends, he thinks spending time with his wife is important, and that competition and winning are important to him. Mr. Jones' answer opens up an avenue for the board to explore how he reacts to disappointment, how he is able to articulate his feelings and reactions, and they'll probably get a good idea of his temperament.

Open-ended questions allow the board to fish around for information, granted, but this is not a negative situation. You should seize these opportunities to open up to the board and give them an idea of how you are as a person.

Obvious Questions

This is the kind of question boards ask when everyone in the room already knows the answer. Example:

Board Member: "Mr. Jones, you were in the military for four years?"
Jones: "Yes sir, I was in the Marines from 1982 until 1986."
Board Member: "Why did you get out?"

The obvious question is used most often as a way to give the applicant a chance to warm up and to be aware of what area the board is about to explore. It's also a way for the board to check up on the information they've been provided. Board members and background investigators can misread or misunderstand information they receive. Understanding this, board members will usually be careful to confirm details with you during the interview.

Fishing Expeditions

The fishing expedition is always a nerve-racking kind of question to answer. You aren't certain why they are asking or where the question came from and they aren't giving out clues. Example:

Board Member: "Mr. Jones, in your application you stated that you've *never* been detained by police. (Usually they will pause a few seconds and then get to the point.) You've *never* been detained?"

If your nerves aren't wracked by this kind of questioning, someone probably needs to check you for a pulse. In the example above, if the applicant has been detained by police and failed to list this on his application then he'll be wondering if the board KNOWS this happened. The odds are sky-high that the board does know the answer before asking the question. If the applicant has never been detained then paranoia is certain to set in. Did someone on his list of references lie to the background investigator? Did someone on the board misread his application? Did.... These questions race through his mind as the board scrutinizes him.

Chances are, the board is simply fishing to see what he'll say. In any event, don't let these questions cause you a dilemma because if you are honest there can be no dilemma. You simply MUST tell the truth at ALL times in an oral board. Your integrity is at stake, your reputation, and, not least of all, your chance to become a trooper is at stake. Don't try to guess at WHY the board is asking a question. Your job is to answer truthfully and openly.

Situational/Ethics Queries

Who doesn't dread these? You hear the words "What would you do if . . ." and your heart pounds wildly. Example:

Board Member: "Mr. Jones, assume you are a state police officer and you are helping another trooper transport several people he has arrested. You see your fellow trooper take a $20 bill out of a prisoner's wallet and put it in his pocket. Your buddy doesn't know you are watching. What do you do?"

Some oral boards are almost exclusively one situational question after another. Other agencies may ask one, then spend the rest of the interview asking you about your past job history. Your best defense here is to decide ahead of time what your ethics are and go with how *you* honestly feel. The only possible right answer is *your* answer. If the board doesn't like what they hear then you may be grilled intensely about your answer; however, you CANNOT assume that you've given the "wrong" answer if the board does begin questioning you hard about your answers. Boards have more than one reason for hammering away at you and it's never safe to assume why they are doing it.

Keep in mind, too, that it's not uncommon on police boards for one board member to be assigned the task of trying to get under an applicant's skin. The purpose is to see if the applicant rattles easily under pressure or loses his/her temper when baited. The person assigned this task is not hard to spot. He/she will be the one you'd love to push in front of a city bus after you've had to answer such questions as: "Why in the world would we want to hire someone like YOU?"

Expect boards to jump on every discrepancy they hear and pick apart some of your comments—all because they want to see how you handle pressure. Not all departments designate a person to perform this function, but someone is usually prepared to slip into this role at some point in the interview.

Role Play Situations

Answering tough questions is stressful enough, but doing it under role play conditions is even tougher. Many departments are using this technique more and more frequently in the oral board setting. A board member will instruct you to pretend you are a trooper and ask you to act out your verbal and/or physical responses. Example:

Board Member: "Mr. Jones, I want you to pretend that you are a state police officer and that you have just pulled over a driver. He becomes uncooperative while you are talking to him and you want him to step out of his vehicle. I want you to stand up now and tell him to get out of his vehicle."

Board members may set up a bit more elaborate role playing scenes for you. Try to enter into these situations with a willingness to participate. Most people are aware that you are not a professional actor or actress so they are not looking for Academy Award performances. Do the best you can. Role playing is used heavily in almost all academies and training situations today so expect to do a lot of role playing during your career as a law

enforcement professional. Shy, reserved people may have difficulty working up enthusiasm for this kind of interaction. Practice how you'd handle this scene and prepare yourself mentally as best you can.

They Can't Ask Me That, Can They?

"They" are the members of the oral board and they can indeed ask you just about any question that comes to mind. Applying for a job in public safety puts you in a different league than the civilian sector applicant. Yes, federal and state laws may prohibit civilian employers from seeking certain information about their applicants. But law enforcement agencies are allowed more freedom of movement within the laws for obvious reasons.

For example, you'll rarely find a space for an applicant's birth date on an application for employment in private industry. This is the result of age discrimination litigation. Law enforcement agencies, as well as other agencies dealing with public safety, need such information to perform thorough background investigations and do not have many of the same restrictions. You will be expected to provide your date of birth and identify your race and your sex before you get very far in the application process for any law enforcement agency. You are applying for a sensitive public safety job and must expect information you may consider highly personal to come to light.

In short, law enforcement agencies can ask you any question that may have a bearing on your mental stability, your ability to do the physical tasks common to state police work, your integrity, honesty, character, and reputation in the community. There's not much left to the imagination after all of this is covered. If some of the questions are probing and perhaps even offensive, it is because you are being held to a higher standard by both the courts who allow these questions to be asked and the departments who want to hire you to protect life and property.

ANSWERS—HOW MANY ARE THERE?

While you are sitting in the interview hot seat you may feel like only two kinds of answers exist—the one you wish you had given and the one you wish you could take back. There isn't a law enforcement officer in uniform today who doesn't have a war story about the one thing he wishes he hadn't brought up in his oral interview board. And this is to be expected. Nerves, pressure, and that random attack of stupid often conspire at the most inappropriate times. To help you be on guard for these moments, let's look at the mysterious "wrong" and "right" answer.

The Wrong Answer

The wrong answer to any question is the answer you think you should say because that's what you've been told the board wants to hear. Do not take well-meant advice from friends or troopers who haven't been before an oral board in the last five years and can't remember much about the one they did go through except that it made them nervous. Boards will often overlook answers they don't "like" if they feel you have good reasons for what you say and if you are being honest with them.

If the board fails you, it will not be because you gave the wrong answer. It will be because you are not the kind of person they are looking for, OR there are some things you need to work on about your life or yourself and the board feels you need some time to work on these matters before they consider you for a job in law enforcement.

The Right Answer

The answers the board wants to hear are the ones only *you* can give. They want *your* opinion, *your* reasons, *your* personal experiences, and they want to know what *you* would do under certain circumstances. No one else matters but you and how you present yourself in the oral interview. If you try to say what you think the board wants to hear you will almost certainly give them a shallow, unsatisfying response to their question.

What DO I Say?

It's not so much *what* you say as *how* you say it. The best way to answer ANY question is with directness, honesty, and brevity. Keep your answers short, but give enough information to fully answer the question. The board won't be handing out prizes for conserving words, but they also don't want to have to pull answers out of you like an old country dentist pulling teeth just so that they can get enough information.

There's a few ways you might want to avoid answering questions. Try not to play "if you ask the question *just* the right way, I'll give you the right answer" with the board. Here's an example:

Board Member: "Mr. Jones, I see you've been arrested once for public intoxication while you were in college? Is that true?
Jones: "No, sir."
Board Member: "Really? That's odd. It says here on page seven that you were arrested and spent the night in the city jail."
Jones: "Yes, well, I wasn't exactly *arrested* because the officer didn't put handcuffs on me.

Don't play word games with the board. You won't win. In this case the applicant clearly knows that the board is aware of his arrest record but he's trying to downplay the incident by trying to duck the question.

Then there's the "you can have the answer if you drag it out of me" and you also want to avoid this technique. For example:

Board Member: "Mr. Jones, tell the board why you left the job you held at Tread Lightly Tire Shop."

Jones: "I was fired."

Board Member: "Why were you fired?"

Jones: "Because the boss told me not to come back."

Board Member: "Why did the boss tell you not to come back?"

Jones: "Because I was fired."

Board Member: "What happened to cause you to be fired?"

Jones: "I was rude."

Board Member: "Rude to whom and under what circumstances?"

You get the picture. This question could have been answered fully when the Board Member asked Jones why he left the tire shop job. The board would prefer that you not rattle on and on when you answer questions, but they would also appreciate a little balance here. This applicant also runs the risk of being labeled a smart alec with this kind of answer. An oral board's patience is usually thin with an applicant who uses this answering technique.

Let's not forget the "you can have any answer but the one that goes with your question" technique. Avoid it, too. Example:

Board Member: "Well, Mr. Jones, we know about some of the things you are good at, now tell us something about yourself that you'd like to improve."

Jones: "I'm really good with people. People like me and find it easy to talk to me for some reason. I guess it's because I'm such a good listener."

If he is a good listener, Mr. Jones didn't demonstrate this quality with that answer. It's important to listen to the question and answer directly. If you duck the question then the board will assume you have something to hide or you are not being honest. If you don't understand how to answer the question, tell the person who asked it that you don't understand. They will be happy to rephrase the question or explain what they want. Be specific and above all, answer the question you are asked, not the one you wish they'd asked instead.

REALITY CHECK

By now, you should have a reasonable idea of what an oral board is looking for and how best to not only survive the experience, but come out ahead on your first board. You've had a lot of material to absorb in this chapter. Read the following scenarios illustrating the wrong way and the right way to tackle an oral interview. As you read, try to put yourself in the shoes of the oral board member who is asking the questions.

Scenario #1

Mary Smith is sitting before her first oral interview board. She is wearing a pair of black jeans, loafers without socks, and a short-sleeve cotton blouse. As the questions are being asked she is tapping her foot against the table and staring at her hands.

Board Member: "Ms. Smith, can you give the board an example of how you've handled a disagreement with a coworker in the past?"

Smith: "Nope. I get along with everybody. Everyone likes me."

Board Member: "I see. So, you've never had a disagreement or difference of opinion with anyone you've ever worked with."

Smith: "That's right."

Board Member: "Well, I see by your application that you were once written up by a supervisor for yelling at a fellow employee. Can you tell us about that situation?"

Smith: "That's different. It was his fault! He started talking to a customer I was supposed to wait on so I told him off."

Now read the second situation.

Scenario #2

Mary Smith is sitting before her first oral interview board dressed in a gray business suit. She is sitting still, with her hands folded in her lap and is looking directly at the person asking her a question.

Board Member: "Ms. Smith, can you give the board an example of how you've handled a disagreement with a coworker in the past?"

Jones: "Yes sir. I can think of an example. When I was working at 'Pools by Polly' I had an argument with a coworker over which one of us was supposed to wait on a customer. I lost my cool and yelled at him. My boss wrote me up because of how I handled the situation."

Board Member: "I see. How do you think you should have handled the situation?"

Smith: "If I had it to do again, I'd take James, my coworker, aside and talk to him about it in private. If I couldn't work something out with him I would ask my supervisor to help out."

Board Member: "What have you done to keep this sort of thing from happening again?"

Smith: "I've learned to stop and think before I speak and I've learned that there is a time and place to work out differences when they come up. I haven't had a problem since this incident."

So, which scenario left the best taste in your mouth? In scenario #1, the applicant is obviously unwilling to accept responsibility for her actions, she isn't showing any evidence that she is mature, and she isn't honest with herself or the board members when she said everyone liked her and she's never had disagreements with coworkers.

On the other hand, in scenario #2, the applicant is able to admit her mistakes and take responsibility for her part in the incident. Although she may have wished she could present herself in a better light, she did illustrate maturity by being honest, open, and straightforward in talking about the disagreement. In scenario #2, the applicant may have had to endure a long, hard interview in order to sell herself, but she was able to articulate what she did to correct a fault.

On the other hand, you can bet she had a very short interview and a "we're not interested, but thanks" from the board in scenario #1. Let's not even talk about the way the applicant was dressed in scenario #1 or her irritating mannerisms!

These two situations may seem exaggerated, but unfortunately applicants all over the country are making these mistakes as you read.

What Do YOU Think?

Since you are all warmed up, read the following situation. Pick from Answer A, B, or C—decide which response you think is most appropriate for the question.

Alfred Wannabe's oral interview board is today at 9 a.m. at the training academy. He's parked in a chair outside of the board room by 8:40 a.m. awaiting THE CALL.

When it comes, Alfred is ushered into the room and introduced to all of the board members. He sits where he's told and waits. It begins.

Board Member: "Mr. Wannabe, what would you like for us to call you this morning?"

Wannabe: (A) "I don't know. It doesn't matter. Alfred is okay, I guess."

(B) "Alfred is fine, sir."

(C) "I go by Al."

Board Member: "Why do you want to be a state trooper?"

Wannabe: (A) "I don't know. I guess because it's fun and you get to help people. I want to be there when somebody needs something."

(B) "I'd like to be a trooper because I'm very interested in the work. I love to be around people. I like the variety of duties. And I like the challenge of trying to figure out what's really going on in a given situation."

(C) "I've always wanted to be a state trooper."

Board Member: "I see. Well, we have a few standardized questions for you and I know a few others will crop up as we go along. First, can you tell us about your personality. What are you like to be around on a social basis?"

Wannabe: (A) "Oh, I don't know. I'm okay, I guess. My friends like me."

(B) "My friends tell me I'm usually fun to be around. I'm not particularly shy. I'd say I'm outgoing. I like meeting new people, talking, and I can be a pretty good listener, too. I am even-tempered. I get mad sometimes, but if I do I get over it quickly. I have a good sense of humor and don't mind being teased as long as I get to tease back."

(C) "I'm easy to talk to, friendly, very social—I like being around lots of people—and I'm laid-back."

Board Member: "I see here that your background investigator found that you once got thrown out of a friend's house during a party because you were picking fights with the other guests. Tell us about this experience."

Wannabe: (A) "Well... that was just that once. I had a little too much to drink I guess. I walked home from there."

(B) "That happened about five years ago in my very early college days. I had just discovered beer and I don't think I handled myself well at all in those days. At that party I kept trying to get everyone to agree to switch the stereo to another station and was quite a jerk about it. My friend asked me to leave so I walked home. I was a jerk again the very next weekend and had to be asked to leave again. That wised me up. I realized I didn't need to be drinking like that so I did something about it."

(C) "Yes, that did happen. I got into an argument with friends over what music we'd listen to. I had been drinking. My host asked me to leave. I did."

Board Member: "What steps have you taken to make sure this type of situation doesn't happen again?

Wannabe: (A) "I guess I just watch how much I drink. I don't go to that guy's house anymore, either."

(B) "I learned to eat before I went to parties where there was alcohol being served and then carried around the same drink for a while. I limited myself to two beers during an evening. I went home happy that way and so did all my friends. I still follow the same rules for myself today."

(C) "I limit myself to two beers at a party and I don't drink much any other time. I'm responsible about the way I drink now."

All of the choices you read are responses candidates have made in oral board situations—not verbatim, but awfully close to it. If you chose Answer (A) for all your responses you will be guaranteed to grate on the last nerve of every board member. It's not hard to see why. Phrases like "I don't know" and "I guess so" and "I think so" tell the listener that the speaker isn't sure of himself. It says the speaker probably has never thought about what you asked and is giving the answer without bothering to think about it now.

Answer A does not give the board much to go on. The answers don't offer explanations, although the open-ended question gives the applicant all the necessary room to do so. The board would be left with a wishy-washy impression of this candidate at best.

If you liked Answer B, you've kept yourself awake for most of this chapter. Answer B shows the applicant has manners, but he doesn't go overboard. He is direct, but not so direct that he comes across as blunt. He has either thought about the kinds of questions that will surface in the interview or he thinks about what he wants to say before he speaks.

He comes across as confident, willing to discuss his past life, and not ashamed to admit mistakes. He also has a detailed explanation for how he's handled the drinking situation and the potential for future problems. It's at this point the applicant needs to be the most vocal. Board members are especially interested in how you handle your life in the present and what you will most likely do in the future.

If Answer C is what you chose, you probably won't blow the interview but if you pass it will be a squeaker. He's not rude, but he walks a thin line. He should elaborate more on how he feels about this career choice because this is one of his opportunities to show the board how well he can express himself. People have different reasons for wanting to go into law enforcement. Some are good and some are marginal, but for the most part this question is designed to warm you up and let the board warm up, too.

It'd be hard to come up with a truly wrong answer for this question, although people have managed to do so. ("I love to shoot guns" would not win extra points here.) The board gets a feel for how you are going to be as an interviewee with this standard question. You don't have to deliver the Gettysburg Address, but give them *something* to go on. By now, you shouldn't have to think about this response anyway. It's a freebie.

Answer C is the type of response quiet, self-assured people often tend to give. They don't use up a whole lot of words and usually answer questions with directness. The danger here is that this applicant may not say enough to convince the board that he will deal well with the public and with other troopers and supervisors.

These kinds of answers will most often force the board to switch to different kinds of questions that will force the applicant into lengthier responses. Don't make them work too hard getting the answers, though, unless you want a *really* short interview.

PULLING IT ALL TOGETHER

Chances are the postal service is looking pretty good right about now. But don't let all of this information become overwhelming. Make yourself step back and look at the big picture. You know what kind of overall impression you are most likely to make. If you don't, you should. And cut yourself a little slack. The people who interview you aren't perfect and have no real desire to hire someone who is, considering they may have to work with you some day.

Keep your sense of humor intact while you're going through this process. No, don't go into the board cracking jokes, but if you can keep your sense of humor close at hand you might actually be able to come out of interview shock long enough to react if the board jokes with you about something. It wouldn't be unusual for this to happen. Most law enforcement personnel like to tease or joke around to relieve stress. Let the board lead the way in this area, though.

Self-confidence is key. Relax, believe in yourself, and let it all come out naturally. If you feel like you are "blowing it" during the interview, show the board your self-confidence by stopping yourself. Take a deep breath and tell them that's not exactly what you'd like to say, then tell them what you'd like to say. Now THAT'S self-confidence. Be firm if a board member tries to rattle your cage. "Firm" doesn't mean inflexible—change your mind if you need to—just don't do it every other sentence. There's always the wishy-washy label to consider—and avoid.

Ready, Set, GO

You are as ready as you'll ever be if you follow these suggestions. There are no secrets to give away when it comes to oral interview boards. You can't change your past, your job history, or your educational status at this point in the process, nor can you change your personality or go back and do a more thorough job on your Personal History Statement. And you can't fake maturity if you are not a mature individual. But you can put your best foot forward, fight for your cause, and be as well-prepared as possible.

Many troopers you see on the road today failed on their first attempt to be hired by their department's oral board and then passed the board after working on shortcomings and correcting problems. Your goal, of course, is to make it through the process on the first try. If that doesn't happen and you decide to try again, you owe it to yourself to come fully prepared the next time around.

If you follow the tips you've read so far you should keep from making many mistakes that tend to eliminate otherwise well-qualified candidates. You will certainly be ahead of the applicant who has the same qualifications you have, but doesn't have a clue as to how to prepare for an oral interview board. Good luck.

SOME FINAL WORDS OF ADVICE

Dr. Rick Bradstreet is a 17-year veteran psychologist for the Austin Police Department in Austin, Texas. He holds a law degree from Stanford University and a Ph.D. in Counseling Psychology from the University of Texas in Austin. His specialty is communication skills and conflict resolution. Throughout his career with APD, Dr. Bradstreet estimates that he's sat on about 250 to 300 oral interview boards and has had plenty of opportunity to observe applicants in oral interviews. He offers the following advice to those who see a law enforcement oral board in their future.

- Make eye contact. Applicants who fail to make eye contact with interviewers can expect a negative reaction from the board. Making eye contact makes the speaker feel like what he or she is saying is being heard and is being taken seriously.
- Sit erect in your chair, but not so stiffly that you appear to be ripe for the woodsman's axe. You should not have the same posture that you would have if you were sitting at home in your living room, yet you want to appear somewhat relaxed and alert.
- Keep your hands in your lap if you have a tendency to wring your hands together when agitated. Wringing hands are generally perceived as signs of nervousness.
- Drumming fingers—try not to drum on the table. Although this behavior is most often interpreted more as a sign of someone who has excess energy and is not necessarily seen as nervous behavior, it can be distracting to those around you.
- Feel free to shift positions periodically. It's perfectly natural to move around as you speak and is expected during normal conversation. An oral board is not meant to be an interrogation so you are not expected to sit frozen in place for the duration.
- Speak up. If a board member lets you know you are mumbling then project your voice. Speaking in a voice so soft that no one can hear you does nothing to enhance the image you want to project—that of a self-confident, take-charge person who knows what you want.
- Focus on explaining how you are as a person and not responding to questions defensively. Once again, this is not an interrogation. Try to have a normal, respectful conversation with the board members and your body language will take on a more natural, confident look.
- Get out of the self-conscious mode. Your goal is to let the board see you and your experiences as unique. Do not try to mold your experiences and answers to questions according to what you "think" the board may want.

C·H·A·P·T·E·R

PSYCHOLOGICAL ASSESSMENT

15

CHAPTER SUMMARY

The psychological assessment, which includes an interview and testing, is an important step in the state trooper selection process. The following chapter describes what to expect and how to prepare for it.

Psychologists can have a fearsome reputation. Whenever there's a terrorist or serial killer, someone sticks a microphone in a psychologist's face to ask: "Why did he do it? What's he like? When will he do it again?" In court, psychologists are asked to describe a stranger's past state of mind: "Was the defendant insane when he committed the murder two years ago?" All of this gives the impression that psychologists have special powers to predict the future and travel the past, and that they can make accurate diagnoses of people they haven't even met. The media enjoy this dramatic image, and play it up—which makes many people believe it.

But the truth is psychologists are neither fortune tellers nor mind readers. They are just skilled professionals who make educated guesses about people, recognizing that they cannot know everything about anyone. They try to produce fair evaluations based on their training and experience and all the available information.

During your assessment it may be helpful to remember that, more than anyone else, psychologists recognize that everyone has weaknesses and makes mistakes (including themselves). In fact, they're less interested in your specific mistakes than in how you handled them—for example, did you learn from them, keep repeating them, and/or blame them on other people?

The point of the psychological assessment is not to criticize or "nail" you; no one expects you to be perfect or even wonderful. Your value as a human being is not on the line here. The goal is only to discover whether your individual pattern of good and bad points matches the profile of most state police officers, which says nothing about how successful you may be in other areas and careers.

PSYCHOLOGICAL TESTING

Testing is part of the assessment process. Most state police departments use some form of the Minnesota Multiphasic Personality Inventory (MMPI), which has 560 simple true/false questions, together with perhaps one other, shorter test. Both are designed to produce a general psychological profile and to detect extremes in attitudes and behaviors. The results may or may not be explained to you, depending on the policies of the department; explanations are very time-consuming and thus impossible to do for everyone.

You cannot study for a psychological test. Besides, you already know the subject matter better than anyone else. You are the world's foremost expert on your own feelings, attitudes, and behaviors, and that's what the testing is about. But while you can't study, there are ways to prepare yourself for it.

One is to remember that testing is only one piece of the picture. You've already filled out a lengthy application and had a background check and probably at least one interview—if you were totally unfit for law enforcement work, you wouldn't have gotten this far!

If the test results raise any questions, your meeting with the psychologist enables you to answer them face-to-face. So try to relax as much as possible, since tension can make it difficult to concentrate (a few deep breaths will help).

It is crucial to be honest in your answers. Don't try to figure out the "right" answer or what each question is getting at. The tests are designed to make this difficult, so you'll only waste time and make yourself more nervous in the process. If you fake your answers, someone is sure to notice (you won't add up right). Besides, if you don't give a true picture of yourself, you may begin a career for which you are poorly suited. And this is not in anyone's best interest, least of all yours.

THE PSYCHOLOGICAL INTERVIEW

It's important to show up for your interview on time and neatly dressed. Respond politely to the questions, but don't volunteer too much information—this is not a social event where you can get loose and friendly. The psychologist (or psychologists—some departments use a team) may spend a few initial moments breaking the ice, but the rest of the 60–90 minutes will be focused and business-like.

It may feel strange to discuss personal things with strangers. It's almost like going to a medical doctor, where you may feel embarrassed about sharing certain information, but must do it for your own good. In the same way, being evasive or defensive in the psychological interview will not do you any good at all.

And yes, you are expected to be nervous. Who wouldn't be? This is a hurdle you have to jump on the way to your goal. At some time in their lives, most people wonder whether they're crazy or not, and you may be afraid that this psychologist will finally confirm it.

Even though it's a myth, that all-powerful, all-seeing shrink image may come to mind. For these and other reasons, it's normal to be nervous. And if you are, it's a good idea to admit it, for this shows honesty and mature self-acceptance. If you are nervous and try to deny it, this suggests a lack of confidence and a tendency to lie, neither of which will gain you any points.

Remember that the psychologist who interviews you is not interested in your full history, only what's relevant to being a state trooper. And don't be surprised if the questions are more personal than in other job interviews you've had. One simple reason is that this job comes with a gun—in other words, when public safety is on the line, the courts allow interviewers to get really nosy.

So you may be asked about your childhood, relationships/marriage(s), and military and high school experiences. Expect questions about which supervisors you liked and didn't like on jobs you've had; this shows how you deal with authority. If you've jumped around from job to job, but there were good reasons for it, be ready to explain them if asked.

Of course you'll be asked why you want to be a state trooper. It's easy to tell a good answer from a bad answer on this one. Good answers: "I want to help people." "I want a secure job with a pension." "My relative (friend) is a cop and I think the work is interesting." Bad answers: "I want to have power over people." "I like excitement and danger." "I can't wait to put all those jerks in jail." Answers that are rehearsed or not really "you" will be obvious, so, once again, just be honest.

Last but certainly not least, don't try too hard to sell yourself. Nervousness is fine, but desperation is not. If you are right for this profession, you must be able to meet challenges with confidence—including the challenge of a brief psychological assessment.

INDEX

INDEX

Tell Us What You Think!

We hope that the information in this book gives you the edge you need in your job search. To help us do our job even better, we would appreciate your taking a few minutes to answer the brief questions below. PLEASE PRINT OR TYPE YOUR RESPONSES. Thank you for your time — and good luck in your career search!

The title of this book is _____

The most helpful part of this book is _____

This book would be even more helpful if it included information on _____

Other jobs or careers of interest to me are

1. _____   3. _____

2. _____   4. _____

How did you find out about this book?

❏ Ad (appearing in _____)   ❏ Recommended to me

❏ Guidance counselor/career counselor   ❏ Other (please explain) _____

I am currently

❏ A student (level: _____)   ❏ Employed (job title: _____)

❏ Other (please explain) _____

Your Name _____

Street Address _____

City _____ State _____ Zip Code _____

Phone Number _____

Your Age _____

Name of a friend who would be interested in LearningExpress products

Name _____

Street Address _____

City _____ State _____ Zip Code _____

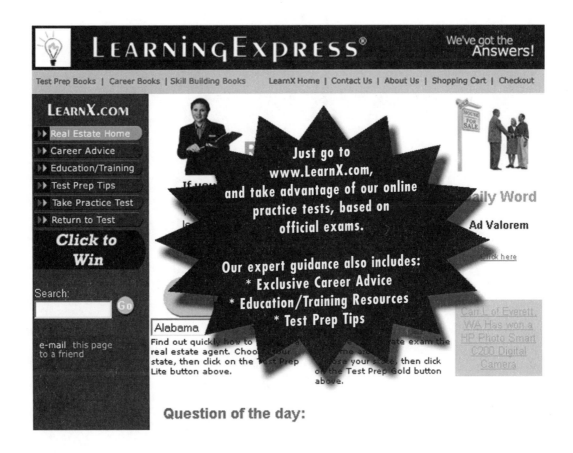

Order Form

CALIFORNIA EXAMS
___ @ $35.00   CA Allied Health
___ @ $35.00   CA Corrections Officer
___ @ $35.00   CA Firefighter
___ @ $20.00   CA Law Enforcement Career Guide
___ @ $35.00   CA Police Officer
___ @ $30.00   CA Postal Worker
___ @ $34.95   CA Real Estate Sales Exam
___ @ $35.00   CA State Police
___ @ $18.95   CBEST (California Basic Educational Skills Test)

NEW JERSEY EXAMS
___ @ $35.00   NJ Allied Health
___ @ $35.00   NJ Corrections Officer
___ @ $35.00   NJ Firefighter
___ @ $20.00   NJ Law Enforcement Career Guide
___ @ $35.00   NJ Police Officer
___ @ $30.00   NJ Postal Worker

TEXAS EXAMS
___ @ $18.95   TASP (Texas Academic Skills Program)
___ @ $32.50   TX Allied Health
___ @ $35.00   TX Corrections Officer
___ @ $35.00   TX Firefighter
___ @ $20.00   TX Law Enforcement Career Guide
___ @ $35.00   TX Police Officer
___ @ $30.00   TX Postal Worker
___ @ $29.95   TX Real Estate Sales Exam
___ @ $30.00   TX State Police

NEW YORK EXAMS
___ @ $15.95   CUNY Skills Assessment Test
___ @ $30.00   New York City Firefighter
___ @ $25.00   NYC Police Officer
___ @ $35.00   NY Allied Health
___ @ $35.00   NY Corrections Officer
___ @ $35.00   NY Firefighter
___ @ $20.00   NY Law Enforcement Career Guide
___ @ $30.00   NY Postal Worker
___ @ $35.00   NY State Police

MASSACHUSETTS EXAMS
___ @ $30.00   MA Allied Health
___ @ $30.00   MA Police Officer
___ @ $30.00   MA State Police Exam

ILLINOIS EXAMS
___ @ $25.00   Chicago Police Officer
___ @ $25.00   Illinois Allied Health

FLORIDA EXAMS
___ @ $32.50   FL Allied Health
___ @ $35.00   FL Corrections Officer
___ @ $20.00   FL Law Enforcement Career Guide
___ @ $35.00   FL Police Officer
___ @ $30.00   FL Postal Worker

REGIONAL EXAMS
___ @ $29.95   AMP Real Estate Sales Exam
___ @ $29.95   ASI Real Estate Sales Exam
___ @ $30.00   Midwest Police Officer Exam
___ @ $30.00   Midwest Firefighter Exam
___ @ $18.95   PPST (Praxis I)
___ @ $29.95   PSI Real Estate Sales Exam
___ @ $25.00   The South Police Officer Exam
___ @ $25.00   The South Firefighter Exam

NATIONAL EDITIONS
___ @ $20.00   Allied Health Entrance Exams
___ @ $14.95   ASVAB (Armed Services Vocational Aptitude Battery): Complete Preparation Guide
___ @ $12.95   ASVAB Core Review
___ @ $19.95   Border Patrol Exam
___ @ $12.95   Bus Operator Exam
___ @ $14.95   Catholic High School Entrance Exams
___ @ $14.95   Federal Clerical Exam
___ @ $14.95   Pass the U.S. Citizenship Exam
___ @ $14.95   Police Officer Exam
___ @ $12.95   Postal Worker Exam
___ @ $12.95   Sanitation Worker Exam
___ @ $18.95   Treasury Enforcement Agent Exam

NATIONAL CERTIFICATION & LICENSING EXAMS
___ @ $20.00   Cosmetology Licensing Exam
___ @ $20.00   EMT-Basic Certification Exam
___ @ $20.00   Home Health Aide Certification Exam
___ @ $20.00   Nursing Assistant Certification Exam
___ @ $20.00   Paramedic Licensing Exam

CAREER STARTERS
___ @ $14.95   Administrative Assistant/Secretary
___ @ $14.00   Civil Service
___ @ $14.95   Computer Technician
___ @ $14.95   Cosmetology
___ @ $14.95   Culinary Arts
___ @ $14.95   EMT
___ @ $14.95   Firefighter
___ @ $14.95   Health Care
___ @ $14.95   Law Enforcement
___ @ $14.95   Paralegal
___ @ $14.95   Real Estate
___ @ $14.95   Retailing
___ @ $14.95   Teacher
___ @ $14.95   Webmaster

To Order, Call TOLL-FREE: 1-888-551-JOBS, Dept. A040

Or, mail this order form with your check or money order* to:

LearningExpress, Dept. A040, 20 Academy Street, Norwalk, CT 06850

Please allow at least 2-4 weeks for delivery. Prices subject to change without notice   *NY, CT, & MD residents add appropriate sales tax*

LEARNINGEXPRESS®